Praise for *How to Fall in Love*

'*A wonderful handbook on relationships, which requires you to be brave, dig deep and face your fears about falling in love.*'
Suzy Greaves, Editor-in-Chief, *Psychologies*

'*Poignant, intimate, shockingly honest and inspiring. Katherine Baldwin is a high-flyer who has found a new, more beautiful way to fly. And with this practical, insightful book, she invites you to do the same. A wonderful, heartfelt journey.*'
Tricia Walker, Acclaimed Book of the Year Author of *Benedict's Brother*

'*I loved reading* How to Fall in Love. *Even though I'm now married, I had lots of light bulb moments about why I'd been attracted to so many unsuitable men in the past. I wish I'd had this book in my thirties when I was looking for love! Katherine writes in such an engaging way and reading about her personal experiences helped me to make sense of my own relationship history. The step-by-step process she shares in the book is transformative and I'd certainly recommend this book to any of my single friends who are looking for a loving, meaningful relationship.*'
Nicola Humber, Author of *Heal Your Inner Good Girl*

'How to Fall in Love *is so much more than a self-help book. It is a beautiful, bold and sincere memoir. This book has given me more than hope. It has reinforced my own journey.*'
Tatiane Lima, Author of *Menina Pra Casar*

Amazon reader reviews

'Such a beautiful book, written in a warm, non-condescending tone. Katherine is wonderfully open and honest which makes it very relatable and moving (I cried at least once). I loved the structure, genuinely useful recommendations and practical suggestions. Can't recommend it enough to anyone who (like myself) struggles with relationships and wants to understand why and how to change that.'

'An inspiring and honest reflection on the pitfalls of dating and the need to re-evaluate expectations. A must-read for both men and women.'

'As the years roll on, it can seem as if you'll never meet the right one. I was beginning to assume there was some secret to falling in love that I just wasn't party to. But reading Katherine's book has given me hope and inspiration. Katherine explains that falling in love is possible. By following her common sense tips and making some mindset changes, we can all grasp the opportunities for love.'

'For anyone who is on a journey to understanding more about themselves, the choices they make in their romantic relationships, exploring perhaps where things have gone wrong in the past and what strategies might help when making healthy choices in the future, this is the book for you. I've read a lot of self-help titles over the years and you take a little something from all of them but Katherine Baldwin's How to Fall In Love, *I read cover to cover and found myself, by the end of it, falling in love.'*

'*Brilliant book, beautifully written with such honesty and straight from the heart. Fascinating insight into ourselves, love, relationships and self-awareness, with so many truths that all of us can relate to and reflect upon. Loved it.*'

'*This is exactly what I needed to read. I totally related to Katherine's experiences and feel so much more positive going forward in my life after gaining some wisdom from her.*'

'*A wonderfully written book full of practical common sense advice and inspirational words of wisdom which may help us all to steer along a more fulfilling journey through life, whatever one's current relationship status or life experiences.*'

'*A great read, full of personal feelings and soul. Whether you're in a relationship or not, the advice within is valuable and inspiring.*'

'*I related to pretty much everything Katherine wrote about and it's given me some solid guidance for future relationships.*'

'How to Fall in Love *is the definitive guide to creating the life and love you want, complete with spiritual and practical advice on how to get there. Beautifully written and honest to the core, this book is the one I wish I'd had when I started out in adult life.*'

How to fall in love

A 10-step journey to the heart

Katherine Baldwin

Soul & Surf

For my inner child.
You have a voice. Enjoy it.

And for Tricia.
Thank you.

About the author

Katherine Baldwin is a writer, journalist, coach and speaker. She writes and speaks from the heart about her journey of transformation, including how she recovered from an eating disorder, challenged self-destructive patterns, learned to love herself and eventually fell in love in her forties.

As a coach, Katherine helps women and men understand why they're single, navigate the world of dating and relationships and fall in love. She also coaches people to make major life transitions and fulfill big dreams, as she has done. As a speaker, she encourages people to learn to manage their emotions in healthy ways and to live authentically.

Katherine's writing has been published in the national media, including in *Red*, *Psychologies*, *The Sunday Times*, the *Guardian*, the *Daily Mail*, *Easy Living* and *The Huffington Post*. She has also appeared on national television and radio

Previously, Katherine worked as a foreign correspondent in Mexico and Brazil for the global news agencies Bloomberg and Reuters before moving back to Britain to work as a political correspondent for Reuters, based in the Houses of Parliament.

Katherine lives by the sea in Dorset with her fiancé.

Contents

Preface

It's a year since I first sat down to write this book, almost to the day.

At the start of 2017, I finally got over myself. I got over my fear, my self-doubt, my procrastination and my perfectionism. I cleared my mind and my diary of distractions, switched my phone and wifi off and committed to my dream of publishing a book.

I wrote *How to Fall in Love* in a month.

I had been struggling to write a different book for a few years but I kept getting lost with it and I didn't set aside the time to find my way. This book, however, pretty much wrote itself. I knew exactly where I was going and what I wanted to say. I was on a mission. I felt inspired. And I gave my writing the time and space it deserved.

It's amazing what happens when we value ourselves enough to prioritise our dreams. We begin to blossom and flourish, in more ways than we could have imagined.

That's certainly been my experience. So much has happened since I published this book, which is why I'm back with this second edition.

The biggest development is that I'm now engaged. I wrote in the introduction to the first edition that, 'My partner and I are not married yet, but I believe we will be when the time is right'. One week after that edition went to print, my partner proposed up a mountain in the French Alps and we now have a wedding date. I couldn't have come up with a better marketing tool if I'd tried – an engagement just days after I released a book of relationship advice – only his proposal wasn't planned. He took me completely by surprise. He says he surprised himself too. You can read about our high-altitude engagement in Chapter 11. This new chapter is a story rather than a step – the story of what happened when I truly committed to my heart's desires. As is often the case with me, it's not a straightforward one.

It's also been a big year for my work. I've brought this book to life through courses, seaside retreats, workshops and coaching. I have plans to run workshops and retreats abroad and to deliver my message in Spanish and Portuguese, languages I used in my former role as a foreign correspondent, which reminds me that nothing is ever wasted.

There have been times, over this past year, when I've had to pinch myself. I used to write about politics in an airless office in the Houses of Parliament, feeling my soul go to sleep every time I switched my computer on. I now lead mindful morning walks and letting go rituals on the beach and help wonderful women, and a few willing men, move forwards on their journey to self-love, self-esteem and a healthy relationship. I get to witness people making positive changes in their lives and going after long-neglected dreams. It's a real privilege and I'm incredibly grateful. I'm especially grateful to those who have put their faith and trust in me and who've come on my retreats or joined my groups. You can hear some of their thoughts at the end of this book.

My story is proof that we can change. We can change our lives, our relationship patterns and our careers if we really want to. Hold on to that thought as you begin working through the 10 steps that follow.

Change, as we all know, requires courage.

Writing this book required huge amounts of courage, which I found deep inside myself and also at the beach – a place where I connect to something greater than myself, something unchanging. I suggest ways to find your courage in the first chapters of this book.

Anger and frustration also motivated me to write. I'd had enough of watching other people publish their books and pursue their purpose, while I stayed silent, too scared to make a noise. My frustration finally trumped my fear of getting it wrong or of being ridiculed and judged.

But my anger and frustration extended beyond my desire to write. I also felt angry every time friends or strangers shared their relationship difficulties or dating disasters, because I heard myself in their troubles and believed I knew where they were going wrong. I felt frustrated every time an intelligent, independent woman told me she had fallen for a guy with a girlfriend, been ditched by a commitment-phobe or had missed out on her dream of biological motherhood because she couldn't find someone to love in time. This frustration continues to drive my work and it has fuelled the second edition of this book. I believe more than ever that my story can make a difference to people's lives and I'm determined that more people should hear it.

Anger and frustration have motivated me to write before.

My anger at the punishing way I had treated my body for most of my adult life led me to launch my first blog,

Just As I Am – An Experiment in Self-Acceptance, back in 2011. My frustration and confusion at turning 40 as a single woman with no children inspired much of my writing on my subsequent blog, *From Forty With Love*, where I still post today.

I found blogging both freeing and therapeutic right from the start. As I poured out my heart and transferred my mostly unedited thoughts onto the screen, I connected to my feelings and explored my pain. As I received comments from readers who shared my troubles, I felt less alone. Through writing, I allowed myself to be vulnerable, to get in touch with my truth and to share it with the world.

I also saw my unhealthy patterns and negative beliefs staring back at me from the computer screen – recorded in nearly six years' worth of blogs. I saw how I kept falling for unavailable and unsuitable men or dismissing the good guys who wanted to commit. Seeing my patterns on the page gave me added impetus to change them. I saw my dreams written in black and white on my blog – my longing to move out of London and live by the sea and my desire to be in a relationship. Then, a few years later, I blogged about how I had made those dreams come true, writing from the home I had bought with my partner on the Dorset coast. I softened through my writing too. I got comfortable with talking about love, which made it easier to say 'I love you' out loud.

Writing has changed my life. It has helped me to make sense of my story and to use my past to make better choices in the here and now. It has also led me to my purpose. It's helped me to turn my pain into passion and to use my life experience to benefit others.

That is my intention with this book.

Introduction

I was 43 before I fell in love and it was nothing short of a miracle. I'd loved before, cared deeply for men, and I'd been infatuated and obsessed but I hadn't ever been *in love*, not like this.

I didn't think I'd ever get here. I watched friends and relatives fall in love, get married and have families. Everywhere I went people seemed to be partnering up. I used to look at them with bemusement. How on earth did they find someone to be with? How did they manage to choose? And how did some of them dare to get married a second or third time around? Once seemed a big enough challenge.

I developed a habit of staring at the wedding rings on people's fingers – and not just to find out if a man might be single. How did people do it? How did they tie the knot? I didn't understand. It felt alien to me. I felt like I was from a different planet.

That's not to say I didn't have relationships. I had plenty of them, beginning in my teens. I had brief encounters, short relationships and a relationship that lasted more than four years. I had periods of singleness too, but the truth is I never stopped hoping. I guess, deep down, I always wanted to be in love, even if love was elusive.

My relationships all ended. There was always a reason to leave or a reason why it wasn't going to work out. Maybe I just haven't met the right guy yet, I thought, as I moved on to the next one or took some time out.

Then, in my early thirties, I was forced to go on a journey of self-discovery – a deep exploration of my past and of my inner make-up. I began to understand who I was at my core and why I behaved as I did in relationships, romantic and otherwise. I began to see how much I disliked myself and how much I was harming myself with my punishing behaviours and unhealthy patterns. I started to understand how lost I was and to realise that I needed to find a new path, a more loving, nurturing and compassionate way of being. I also saw that I needed to anchor myself, to find a power greater than myself to hold on to.

I began a process of personal transformation – similar to the one I describe in this book – and I came out the other side. I grieved the losses of my past and healed my wounds. I challenged my thinking and learned to act in my best interests in many areas of my life.

I softened and grew stronger inside at the same time. I became a more complete person. I developed confidence in myself and got clearer about what I wanted out of life. I became more resilient and more able to risk my heart because I knew I could survive endings. I did some of the growing up I had neglected to do as a child. I matured emotionally.

The journey is ongoing, but today I am happily in love. I am now one of those women I used to look at in bemusement, wondering how on earth she managed to find a guy and form a relationship. I am in one of those couples I used to stare at as they walked past me, arm-in-arm. I am engaged to a wonderful man and we are planning our wedding.

I now understand why people want to be in a relationship. I don't think I ever really got it before. Why take that risk? Why lose your freedom? Why compromise? Why put up with someone else's funny ways? But I get it now. I appreciate the joy of being in a partnership, even with its inevitable ups and downs. I wouldn't change it for the world. And I'm confident my partner and I will be able to work through any troubles that come our way. There is enough love to keep us strong and I'm more mature than I was.

I did an extraordinary amount of work on myself to get here. I recovered from addictive and compulsive behaviours and from dysfunctional relationship patterns and I spent many hours in therapy sessions. I studied child and adult development as part of a diploma in counselling and psychotherapy skills and I read scores of self-help books. I tried and failed to have relationships many times and I learned my lessons, very slowly, two steps forward, one step back at times.

Along the way, I benefited hugely from hearing other people's experiences. I'd now like to see if my story could benefit you. More than that, I feel compelled to share my journey to love. As the poet Rumi said: 'Everyone has been made for some particular work and the desire of that work has been put in every heart'. This book was put in my heart.

Before I go any further, however, let me just say that I don't have the answers. I don't know for sure why you're single, why none of your relationships have worked out or why you can't meet someone you find attractive who is also available. I have my theories, based on my experiences, but I don't actually know.

But you do. You have your answers, just as I had mine.

I used to think that someone else had the answers for me and I've sought a lot of help. But the most useful books, the best therapists, the wisest gurus and the kindest friends haven't told me what to do. They've shown me how to find the answers inside myself. They've helped me to connect to my intuition, trust my instinct, make my own mistakes and learn from them.

That's my goal with this book. I'm here to help you connect to your truth and to encourage you to take healthy risks based on self-awareness and sound discernment. That said, I am going to offer some suggestions, based on my own personal catalogue of bad dates, painful break-ups, crazy fantasies, wasted years and lessons learned.

Who this book is for

How to Fall in Love is a dating and relationships guide with a difference. It's for women and men who are looking for more than a few tips on how to write an appealing online profile or where to meet singletons, although I do touch on those topics. It's for people who are willing to go deeper, to reflect on the reasons for their singleness and to embrace the prospect of change. So if you're struggling to understand why you've reached your age or life stage without managing to find a partner or make a relationship work, this book is for you. And if you've ever heard the words, 'You're a real catch. I can't understand why you're still single' or if you've said them to yourself, you're in the right place.

This book is also for people who no longer believe they're a catch and who've lost faith in their ability to meet someone and to form a healthy, loving relationship. It's for women and men who have been alone for a long time and for those who are looking for love after separation, divorce or being widowed.

I'm not here to argue that relationships are for everyone or that singleness is the wrong way to be. That's for you to decide. I'm here to get you thinking about the potential reasons for your single status and the steps you can take to change your circumstances if love is your goal.

How to Fall in Love isn't just for single readers, however. It's for anyone who wants to connect with the desires of their heart, understand themselves better, improve their relationships, transform their circumstances or take a leap of faith in any area of their life, and who is looking for the courage and the inspiration to do so.

What if you still want children?

If you're a single woman living in what I call 'the baby gap' – that period of excruciating uncertainty that kicks in when you start to realise you might want to have children but your fertility window is closing fast – I know how you're feeling. I get your confusion, frustration, panic and pain. I understand your fear that you might miss out on a big dream and on one of life's great miracles. I've been there. I spent my early forties feeling the same. In fact, the baby gap and the motherhood dilemma are the focus of another book I still hope to finish.

There is no easy answer here. In our careers, we set ambitious goals and we achieve them through hard work and determination but having a family isn't like that. Even with the advances of science, with IVF, egg freezing and egg donorship, nothing is guaranteed. Even if you pursue adoption, you can never be sure you'll tick all the necessary boxes and bring home a child. Having a family is out of our control.

However, if you're sure you want a child above all else and you're running out of time, try and make a positive choice. Explore the multitude of options of having a baby or adopting on your own. Do your research. Speak to people who've done it. Then take some action.

But if you're not ready to be a single parent or if your heart is telling you that's not your path, commit to working the steps in this book or to finding other ways to transform yourself so that you are able to meet a partner and fall in love as soon as you can. You may find you are able to make a relationship work in time to have a family. I'm not making any promises, but surely it's worth a try? Or you may find the steps in this book help you to reassess your priorities. You may discover another dream or, once you're in love, you may find there's nothing missing from your life, which is how I feel most of the time.

If you feel ambivalent about having children, I can relate to that too. You'll find references to ambivalence throughout this book and a blog post in Appendix I, in which I try to work through my own mixed feelings about motherhood.

If you have definitely missed out on being a parent and you are grieving that loss, give yourself the space to feel your feelings and then, when you're ready, try the steps in this book. Love and partnership may help to soothe your pain.

Why 10 steps?

There are 10 steps in this book and you may be wondering where that number comes from. As with other self-help books, the number is somewhat arbitrary. I could have split the steps into mini-steps or tacked another few steps on the end. However, these are the steps that came to me as I scribbled my plan for this book on a few sheets of A4 one January morning in 2017. And these are the steps I worked through with a small group of women who joined my first 'How to Fall in Love' coaching programme around the same time. That programme is still running and the 10 steps are at the heart of my workshops and retreats. You may want to combine the steps in this book with other healing, coaching or personal development work you are doing or you may want to skip through some steps that don't resonate with you. Take what you like and leave the rest.

How to use this book

As you read this book, you will notice there are sections where I ask you to pause and reflect. I have also included some further reflections and suggested actions at the end of each step. I hope you can make space in your schedule to do some of the work. But if you're anything like me, you won't pause and reflect as you read. You might answer some questions in your head but you won't stop to pick up a pen and paper. If that's the case, can I suggest you return to the beginning of the book once you've reached the end, work through the questions and choose the actions that feel right for you? You have invested in yourself by buying this book so invest in yourself further by doing the work. You could also find a friend to go on this journey with you or you could join one of my groups, coaching programmes or retreats and get support that way. I'll remind you of the importance of doing the work in my closing words.

My truth

This book is my truth, or as much of my truth as I feel able to share while honouring the memory or privacy of others. If I have omitted any aspects of my story, it is out of respect for the people I love.

You will read about some concepts in these pages that I have come across on my personal development journey – concepts from the worlds of psychology, psychotherapy, spirituality, faith and addiction recovery. I have written about these concepts as I understand them and as they relate to my experience. Others may interpret them differently.

Similarly, where I have written about past experiences or about previous relationships, romantic or otherwise, I have drawn on my own recollections of those experiences and relationships. Other people may remember them in a different way.

A note on language

I wrote this book more or less as I speak because I was working to a tight deadline and I found it easier that way. That means the language I've used, for the most part, is that of a heterosexual woman who is looking for a male partner. I have also directed my writing primarily towards women because that is the world I know. Now and then I have varied my pronouns but not often. I hope by writing in this way I have not excluded male readers or those seeking same-sex relationships because I do believe this book is relevant to all. Please do not be put off by my use of pronouns.

You will find references to God in these pages. As you'll read in the early chapters of this book, I've been on a spiritual journey and I've settled on a faith that works for me.

You will have your own path and your own beliefs. If you are looking to connect with something greater than yourself, please use whatever term or concept you're comfortable with – the Universe, Mother Nature, Higher Power, Love, God and so forth – or perhaps you prefer the idea of connecting with your Higher Self or your inner voice.

Time to flourish

Finally, this book isn't just about dating, relationships and romantic love. It's about learning to flourish in all areas of your life. It's about thriving rather than surviving. It's about trusting yourself, taking healthy risks, identifying your dreams and going for them.

By writing and publishing this book, I am doing all of those things. I sincerely hope it will help you to do the same.

Chapter 1

Step inside

'What lies behind you and what lies in front of you pales in comparison to what lies inside of you'
Ralph Waldo Emerson

'Step Inside Love', sang my fellow Liverpudlian Cilla Black in 1968.

I invite you to do the same.

I invite you to slow down, sit quietly, look inside and connect to yourself on a deep level.

This is where our journey to love begins.

Why do we start here? Well, I believe one of the reasons I took so many wrong turns on my dating and relationship journey – and took so long to find love – is that I was disconnected from my feelings.

I was looking to form romantic relationships with others without a clear understanding of who I was on the inside and without a healthy relationship with myself. The idea that you have to love yourself first before you can love another may sound like a bit of a cliché, but for me, it turned out to be true.

In my case, the disconnection was extreme. I trust yours

isn't quite so severe. Nevertheless, I want to begin by sharing my story in the hope that you can relate to some elements of it and that it might help you identify if or where you have a faulty connection.

My story

Throughout my teens, twenties and early thirties, I was completely detached from myself. This was deliberate, or rather it was a deliberate act on the part of my subconscious mind – that part of our brain that stores all our past life experiences and wants to protect us from hurt.

As a young girl, I found ways to disconnect from myself because the feelings lurking beneath the surface were too painful to feel. I was a sensitive child and my heart broke when my parents split up and my dad moved out. I was about eight at the time and I felt confused, lost, afraid and insecure. I also felt guilty because I thought what was happening was somehow my fault. My world had been rocked and I didn't know what was coming next.

Those feelings were overwhelming at times so I looked for ways to avoid, numb or soothe them, as well as to restore some sense of control because everything seemed to be unravelling.

Food was my first crutch. It became my secret friend and security blanket. In my early teens, I began starving, bingeing and compulsively exercising to change the way I felt and to control how I looked. But as I progressed through adolescence, that cycle of binge eating and starving took control of me. Once I started eating, I couldn't stop. I gained weight and hated myself.

I drank to excess too, from the moment I first went to

the pub with my friends, aged 14. I used alcohol as an escape and a way to anaesthetise the grief and loss I was experiencing. I also drank to feel more confident and secure in myself.

At school, I studied and worked obsessively, with a perfectionism that was crippling at times. I became head girl, racked up A grades in my exams, captained sports teams and topped it all by winning a place at Oxford University.

After I got my degree, I bought a plane ticket to Sydney with the proceeds of a summer job and began travelling on my own for two years, touring Australia, New Zealand, Fiji and the United States. I shared flats, dorms and lifts with other travellers but food and alcohol were my only constant companions.

I arrived in Mexico in 1995 and began working as a news journalist, a career I had wanted to pursue ever since my final year of school when I watched Kate Adie report for BBC TV from China's Tiananmen Square on the mass killing of students.

I climbed the career ladder, moved to Brazil for a few years and then, aged 31, landed the coveted role of UK political correspondent for the global news agency Reuters.

I worked out of an office in the Houses of Parliament, just beneath Big Ben, went to news conferences and drinks parties in 10 Downing Street and travelled the world with then Prime Minister Tony Blair. I was there when Blair met with George W. Bush to prepare the way for the Iraq war and when he visited British troops in the Iraqi desert after the fall of Baghdad.

Far from increasing my confidence, however, my elevated work status brought with it a chronic case of imposter syndrome. I never felt good enough and I was constantly afraid I'd be found out as a fraud.

So I ate.

I ate because my work could never be perfect. I ate to run from the fear of making a mistake. I binged on sugar to boost my energy because I was working so hard and I gorged on bread because I didn't have time to prepare proper meals.

All along, food was my co-pilot and alcohol was in the back seat. The extra layer of fat, which varied in thickness over the years, acted as a protective shield, keeping people and feelings at arm's length, while a steady flow of adrenaline gave me the sense of power I was so lacking and immunised me against hurt.

In the relationship arena, I also swung between extremes. I'd have long periods of singleness or enter into relationships but remain distant and detached, or I'd seek out men who were equally disconnected from their feelings or unavailable in some other way. At other times, I'd be obsessed – high on a fantasy I'd created around some guy I thought was ideal for me, until the bubble burst, of course. Or I'd pursue dramatic and even illicit, adrenaline-fuelled flings that began with fireworks but soon went up in smoke. Words like *moderation* or *middle ground* were not part of my vocabulary.

My hobbies provided no refuge from my emotional extremes. Instead, they fuelled my inner adrenaline junkie. I'd parachute out of planes, bungee jump off bridges, camp alone in dark woods or hike up snowy peaks in old trainers.

I liked risk. I liked to live on the edge. It gave me a buzz and took me away from myself.

Your coping mechanisms

The lengths I went to in order to disconnect from my emotions were extreme, as I mentioned, but I wonder if my experience rings any bells with you.

I wonder if your subconscious mind has sought out ways to keep you detached from your feelings or to block you from having a deep, intimate relationship with yourself (and, as a result, with a partner too).

I wonder if you are eating on your emotions, drinking to excess, working around the clock, exercising compulsively or keeping yourself so busy you don't have time to breathe or to cook.

I know some of you are, because we've met.

My social circles are full of ambitious, high-achieving, successful and busy women. And why not? The opportunities were there for us and we jumped at them, some of us determined to create better lives for ourselves than our parents had had. We excelled at our studies and in our careers. We worked hard, played hard and worked out with gusto. We kept our minds and bodies busy.

I've since discovered that my busyness was an incredibly effective way to avoid my feelings and to ignore what was really going on inside.

I wonder if that's the case for you too.

I was a compulsive doer – always working or running or socialising. No wonder my friends used to call me the Duracell Bunny after the hyperactive pink rabbit on the TV advert. But I've realised that if we keep moving and never sit still, we can't connect to ourselves and we end up avoiding any feelings of loneliness, grief, hurt, disappointment or fear that may be lying beneath the surface.

Isn't this a good thing? After all, why would we want to feel pain? The problem is if we can't feel it, we can't understand where it comes from and that means we can't process it, heal it or learn to deal with it in a healthy way. It stays with us, making us act against our best interests and sabotaging our efforts to form intimate relationships based on self-awareness, emotional maturity, truth and trust.

If we can't connect to ourselves on a deep level, we'll struggle to connect to others or to feel empathy for other people's pain. And the same barrier that keeps the unpleasant feelings at bay will also block us from good feelings, from intimacy and from love.

Similarly, if we pursue the highs and lows of adrenaline-fuelled romantic escapades with unavailable types or live in a fantasy world in which our married work colleague just has to be our Mr Right, we'll never learn to cope with real feelings or with the ups and downs of real-life relationships. We won't mature emotionally or grow up.

This is a great way to stay single.

I believe it's only when we stay still long enough to get in touch with all of our feelings that we can process any past hurts and learn to understand, accept and love ourselves fully. And it's only then that we can do any maturing that we may still have to do and build the solid foundations needed to find love.

That's why stepping inside is the beginning of our journey towards a true, intimate relationship.

Pause and reflect

- Take a moment to reflect on my story. Can you relate to any elements of it?
- Think about any crutches or coping mechanisms you may have used over the years to numb your feelings, escape your pain or cope with imposter syndrome.
- Have you turned to excess food, alcohol, cigarettes, drugs, compulsive work, busyness, punishing exercise, sex or any other substances or behaviours to get by?
- Do you think you might be ready to connect with the feelings you've been hiding from, become more aware of your hurt and process it in healthy ways?

Embracing the emptiness inside

For me, the journey towards self-awareness began in my early thirties. Up until then, I'd been in denial about my eating disorder but when I was about 32, it dawned on me that I had an abnormal relationship with food and with my body and I realised I needed help.

I believe I would have carried on bingeing if I could have done, but something changed – the pain and shame I felt after a binge were now greater than the pain and fear I was trying to avoid, so I had no choice but to stop.

I started attending support groups for people with eating disorders and began seeing a therapist and slowly learned to stop numbing my feelings with food. As I let go of the comfort blanket that had been with me since childhood, I got in touch with the pain, grief, fear and insecurity I'd been hiding from all my life. I began to see that beneath my successful exterior, there was an emotionally immature, frightened child who was terrified of people, of relationships and of love.

As I began to heal, I was advised to find healthier ways to live my life and manage my emotions – to find something else to rely on, some sort of power greater than myself.

I set out on what I can only describe as a spiritual journey. I took baby steps at first, slowing down, rekindling a relationship with the faith I'd known as a child and dipping my toe into meditation. But I was still holding on to some survival tools from my past and I soon realised I would need to let go of all my crutches in order to truly connect to myself.

I wanted to believe I could carry on drinking socially, but hangovers inevitably led to eating binges so the drinking had to stop. I also thought I could continue pounding the pavements and working at my high-adrenaline job but my attempts to do so were brought to an abrupt halt.

I was 34 when my dad died of prostate cancer and his death knocked me for six. I got sick and stopped running – pulling out of the London marathon – but I only took a few weeks off my job, believing the busyness and routine would help me cope with the loss.

On the surface, my strategy worked and I bounced back well. I even began a relationship five months after my dad's death but when my boyfriend and I split up a year later, I was hit by an avalanche of grief.

Around the same time, I reached a crisis point with my work as I realised that the job I'd fought so hard for and that had consumed me for years was stifling my spirit and putting my soul to sleep. As soon as I switched on my computer in that stuffy Reuters office in parliament, a light went out inside me.

The combination of so many raw emotions and the dread I felt around my work became too much to bear. I broke down and got signed off work – 'stress, anxiety, grief, bereavement and depression', the doctor's note said.

I had been forced to slow down. I had been forced to stop.

In the stillness that followed, I came face-to-face with a deep emptiness inside me. This nothingness had been there for years but I'd done an incredible job of running away from it and of filling the hole inside with food, alcohol, achievement, work and male attention.

Late one night, I hit my spiritual rock bottom. I found myself on my knees by the side of my bed sobbing, 'God, if you're there, tell me what's the point?'

There was no thunderbolt, no flash of lightning and no reassuring voice but that moment marked a turning point. I had a choice: I could either give up entirely or commit to a new way of living, to a spiritual path of self-love rather than a punishing, self-harming one.

Fortunately, I'm too stubborn to give up.

A process of transformation

I used to think the feelings would kill me if I allowed them to surface. I used to think the emptiness would swallow me up if I faced it head on. But the most courageous thing I have learned to do is to connect with myself, feel the feelings, embrace the emptiness and love myself through the pain. I believe this has been a fundamental step on my journey to forming a healthy relationship with myself and it has enabled me to mature emotionally so I could be open to meeting a partner and falling in love.

You may not need to feel so much hurt or peer inside any

black holes. You may not need to break down in order to break through. But you may have to slow down a bit, explore who you are at your core and spend some time with yourself.

You may have to let go of some unhealthy habits that are disconnecting you from your feelings, like eating, drinking, smoking, running too far or working too much. You may have to learn to embrace all of you and to love yourself wholeheartedly. You may have to get in touch with your needs and learn to meet them. You may also need to ask others for help or find some form of supportive community, spirituality or faith.

Whatever it is, if you're reluctantly single and you're reading this book, it's likely you're going to have to engage in a process of change or transformation to have the relationship you want.

If you've mastered this connection with yourself or have formed a relationship with a power greater than yourself already, I'd invite you to strengthen that relationship as you move through this book. I know from experience that when it comes to getting to know ourselves, understanding who we are and connecting to our heart, soul, spirit or intuition, we can always go deeper.

Ongoing healing

I have continued to evolve since that dark moment by my bed when I reached out for help. I've become more consistent with my meditation practice and with prayer. I've developed a relationship with God that works for me and I've found fellowship and community to help with my recovery. I've left my all-consuming news journalism job and now work for myself, doing work that's aligned with my authentic self and that feeds my soul, brings me joy and allows me more freedom. I'm by no means cured of all my crazy ways but I have transformed.

This hasn't been easy. It has involved making bold decisions. But I've continued to cultivate the art of moving slowly or sitting still, knowing this connection to myself is a priority. I've swapped the pavement-pounding for Pilates or gentle walks and I now spend more time doing things that make my heart sing, like cycling in the countryside and swimming outdoors.

And, in July 2015, I took the momentous step of moving out of London to the Dorset coast where I walk on the beach and swim in the sea as often as I can.

My life has changed dramatically but the most important change, the change that has enabled me to take risks and to fall in love, has been on the inside.

I've been healing my wounds, understanding my past hurts, identifying my patterns and getting to know who I am without the crutches of food, drink, status, busyness or adrenaline. I've been loving myself and learning to meet my needs. I've been connecting to my intuition and learning to discern what's right for me.

I now notice the tap on my shoulder or the feeling in my gut that's directing me down a certain path or warning me off another and often, if not always, I can muster up the courage to pay attention to my inner voice. If I can't, I accept this journey is about progress, not perfection.

For me, getting to this point has been a long and tortuous process. Sometimes I think I'm a slow learner. Other times, I think I've had a lot to unlearn and learn again.

I believe many of us need to do this inner work in order to

be in the right place to meet a suitable, healthy partner and fall in love. I believe we need to be in touch with our feelings, our heart, our intuition, our patterns and our past hurts in order to make wise choices about whom we date.

If we can connect with ourselves on a deep level, we'll be able to approach dating and relationships with a stronger sense of who we are and what we need and with more resilience, confidence and peace. We'll feel less panic and more acceptance, even if we want children but fear we're running out of time. We'll have the courage to say 'Yes' when we mean 'Yes' and 'No' when we mean 'No'.

We'll save months, perhaps years of our lives because we'll be able to walk away from dead-end relationships, break unhealthy bonds with past loves or ditch obsessions that are holding us back. Best of all, we'll save a whole heap of heartache and pain by being more discerning about whom we open up to. We'll listen to our intuition rather than ignore it. We'll be more aware of our needs and more able to ask for them to be met. We'll feel more complete and therefore we will find emotionally healthy people attractive, rather than dull as we did before – and they will be drawn to us too.

So, if you're looking for love, look no further. Step inside and spend some time with yourself.

Finding your path

Practically speaking, how do we do this? Well, we each need to find our own unique path to self-awareness. We each need to find the best way to connect to ourselves and to our feelings, to hear our intuition and to cultivate peace.

For me, developing a gentle morning routine that prioritises my connection with myself and, in my case, with

God has been key. I start by reading a passage or two from one of the many spiritual or self-help books I've collected over the years. I try to do this even if everything in me wants to check Facebook or look at my email.

Of course, there are days when I have to dash out of the house and don't have time to sit still but if that happens, I try to find a moment later in the day when I can connect.

Next, I practise some form of meditation.

Meditation helps us to access a state of consciousness that is different from being awake, asleep or dreaming. It's a state that brings mental clarity and emotional peace and that gives our bodies deep rest, which enables them to heal. In meditation, our attention is focused inwards rather than outwards on the world.

There are many ways to meditate but in recent years, I've been practising mindfulness meditation – a form of meditation in which you direct your focus to something, like your breath, the feeling of the chair beneath your body or any sounds you can hear. As someone who's always struggled to sit still and calm my mind, I've found this the easiest type of meditation to get my head around.

In the beginning, however, I found any form of meditation excruciating. I resisted it and railed against it, getting angry with myself because I couldn't stop the thoughts or do it right. Sometimes I'd give up halfway through.

The biggest lesson has been that there is no right or wrong way to meditate so I don't need to strive to do it perfectly or beat myself up if I only get a few seconds of peace in a 15-minute slot. Yes, my thoughts keep coming and I mull over all the problems I want to solve but as soon as I remember I'm trying to meditate, I detach from the thoughts, let them flow past and focus back on my breath.

My meditation routine isn't anything fancy or super spiritual. I have a mindfulness app on my phone via which an American lady encourages me to connect to my breath or to notice any sensations in my body. Sometimes, if I'm struggling to connect to myself, I place my hands on my tummy so I can feel the gentle movement of my breath, or over my heart so I can feel its steady beat. This reminds me I'm a human being, rather than a human doing or a human thinking. It brings me back to the present moment.

If you want to find out more, I'd encourage you to check out some of the many books and studies that discuss the mental health benefits of meditation and the science behind it. My own experience is evidence enough for me. I know meditation has made me a calmer, more peaceful and more accepting person. I've discovered a way to sit still, feel more resilient in the face of life's trials and be more courageous when it comes to following my heart.

Pause and reflect

- Do you feel you would benefit from a moment of calm in your day?
- If you already meditate, why not deepen your practice? If you don't, why not start with five minutes, then build up to 15 and then maybe 30?
- If that seems impossible with your schedule – maybe you have young children, elderly parents, a hectic job or all of the above – just take time out for a minute or two each day.

- Why not try it right now? Stop what you're doing, close your eyes and listen to the sound of yourself breathing. Put your hand on your heart, your chest or your tummy and take a deep breath, and another. And smile. That's all it takes to experience a moment of calm.

Sitting with the feelings

When you begin to connect in this way, especially if you've never done it before and you've been busy rushing around, you may notice some unwelcome emotions. As you experience silence and stillness, you may get in touch with feelings of loneliness or pain. Tears may flow.

Don't be alarmed. This isn't a sign you need to stop. These are growing pains. This is you getting in touch with the deep blocks that have held you back for years and sabotaged your relationships. You need to feel these feelings in order to heal them and move forwards. So welcome them. Embrace them. Let the tears come.

If the tears won't stop or you're having extreme feelings, seek support from a counsellor or a therapist. Otherwise, just make sure you love yourself through this process. Take care of yourself, nurture yourself and give yourself plenty of rest. Wrap yourself in a warm blanket, both literally and metaphorically.

These moments of healing are stepping stones on the journey to love.

Everyday mindfulness

As well as having a meditation practice, you can also bring mindfulness into everyday life. You can walk, wash the dishes or brush your teeth in a more mindful way, focusing on what you're doing rather than thinking about what you'll be doing next or trying to work out the solution to a problem in your head. If you're walking, feel the pavement or the grass beneath your feet. Feel the muscles flexing in your legs and listen to your breath flowing in and out of your body.

As you begin this practice, it's important to be aware of the difference between meditation and rumination. I'm a great one for ruminating. Just as cows chew the cud, I can chew over a problem relentlessly, believing that if I think long and hard enough about it, I'll be able to change it or solve it. I'll ruminate while I'm trying to meditate or when I'm out walking but I'm now aware of this and I soon bring my thoughts back to my breath or to the scenery around me.

Sometimes, if I'm not in the mood for sitting still, I take my morning routine with me to the beach. I walk or jog slowly and sometimes swim. Being by the sea brings me peace and joy while swimming or playing in the waves delights the little girl inside me. Often, I'm the only one swimming for as far as the eye can see. I glance out to the horizon and up to the sky and realise I'm a tiny speck on a huge, majestic landscape. This calms my anxiety. The earth will keep turning, the tide will keep flowing in and out and I'll always find a way to resolve whatever problem I'm dealing with. Being in nature grounds me and helps me put things into perspective. It connects me with God. I can also access that feeling of being grounded by hugging trees or walking barefoot on the grass.

What about you? How do you find peace? How do you get in touch with your intuition, your inner voice or a power greater than yourself? Try experimenting with a few things until you find a way to connect to yourself or to the Universe,

Mother Nature, God, a Higher Power, Love or whatever concept works for you. Once you've found something that works, just keep doing it. It's that simple.

Writing and gratitude

As well as physical activities, I also find writing is a wonderful way to connect with my intuition. I've always written, ever since I was a little girl. I've got diaries dating back decades. But it's only in recent years that I've been able to use writing to tap into my feelings and hear the messages of my heart and soul.

I write in notebooks and I've been blogging for six years, letting the words flow straight from my heart and head onto the computer screen. I find this process freeing.

For months now, I've also been writing a gratitude list. I do it most days. I list all the wonderful things in my life: love, my partner, good health, my home, living near the sea, the sunshine, the frost, anything that comes to mind. I also list situations or feelings that aren't quite so positive, things that are bugging me or causing me stress and I give thanks for them too. So my list may include feelings like anxiety or something that is making me anxious, such as an argument, a difficult conversation or money worries.

Writing it all down seems to help me accept it. My issues seem less daunting when I put them down on paper. They become problems to solve in amongst plenty of other good stuff rather than overwhelming difficulties.

One thing I've learned from doing these lists is that my troubles come and go – nothing stays on the list for too long.

You may have other ways of connecting to yourself. Perhaps animals help you find peace, or being with children.

Both have an extraordinary ability to bring us back to the present moment.

Practices like yoga and Pilates are also a great way to learn about the benefits of being more centred and connected. For some, yoga is the first step on a spiritual journey.

Learning to let go

All of these practices help us to let go a little, to surrender and relinquish control.

One of the hallmarks of my single life was my belief that I had to control everything, that I could only rely on myself and that I couldn't be vulnerable or ask for help. Slowly, as I learned to sit still and connect to myself, I began to soften.

Before I began my spiritual journey, there was a hardness to me – a hardness I prided myself on. My favourite song for many years was Simon & Garfunkel's 'I am a Rock'. I liked the idea that I could stay safe behind my armour, that I could build walls or dig a moat to protect myself from further hurt. My past hardness surprises me now, although I understand why the lyrics of that song were my mantra for so long.

Your journey may also require a softening. Perhaps you'll want to open up to those around you, share this new path that you're on with others and talk about the feelings that are coming up.

Perhaps you'll want to challenge yourself to ask for help rather than trying to do everything yourself. Allowing yourself to be vulnerable and to ask for support is risky because you never know whether your request will be met or denied. Some of us are highly sensitive to rejection because of our childhood experiences so we try to avoid it at all costs.

But learning not to take things too personally and to deal with rejection in a healthy way is part of life's journey and it will stand you in good stead as you step out and start dating. You may be surprised when you reach out to others. You may discover your friends or family members are overjoyed that you've asked them for help and it may bring a new closeness to your relationships.

Becoming comfortable with vulnerability and learning to trust others will help you to date and form healthy, loving relationships. And if you're more connected to yourself, you will make better, more loving choices. You will be more aware of your needs and more able to communicate them. You will also be more accepting if you don't get the answers you want and more able to discern whether to stay in a relationship or leave. This goes for all relationships – romantic relationships, friendships, family and work relationships.

Over to you

So why not try to practise mindfulness meditation for a few minutes in the morning every day this week? As you sit in stillness, put your hand on your chest, heart or tummy and listen to your breath. Use a meditation app or play some calming music. Notice how you feel. Do you feel sadness, joy, apprehension or anger? Let the feelings come.

If you have a decision to make, try to listen out for your intuition during or after a period of meditation. Don't expect a booming voice telling you what your next step should be. Just try to sense how you feel.

If answers come to you, notice whether they feel right. Do you feel peaceful or anxious when you think about taking action? You may come away thinking you know which direction to take but then choose not to follow through with it. I've lost count of the number of times I've ignored my inner voice. I'm only human, after all. But notice why you decided to ignore your intuition and what happened as a result. You can then store that memory for next time.

This will increase your awareness and awareness is the first step on the journey to change. You'll be acting more mindfully and more consciously and you'll be laying some firm foundations on which to build a healthy relationship.

If you feel resistance, persevere.

From my experience and from talking to high-achieving women with perfectionist traits, it's the people who need to meditate the most that find it the hardest to do. It's the women who are running the fastest who most need to slow down. So be as determined and persistent with your meditation and self-care as you have been with your career or any other aspects of your life you've invested in. You deserve it.

From this new place of stillness, with a stronger connection to yourself, you can begin the work of strengthening your core and increasing your self-esteem.

We'll look at that in the next step.

Step One: Reflection and action

- Notice if you are connected to your feelings or detached from them.
- Try to identify if you are using unhealthy crutches to manage your emotions and cope with life, such as excess food or alcohol, compulsive work or punishing exercise.
- Explore healthier ways to get by – meditation, a spiritual connection, gentle exercise, time in nature or a supportive community. Take a look at the Resources section at the back of this book for ideas.
- Experiment with mindfulness meditation using simple apps such as Mindfulness or Headspace.

My reflections

Chapter 2

Strengthen your core

*'When the roots are deep there is
no reason to fear the wind'*
African proverb

In the last chapter, you began to explore ways to connect to yourself and to get in touch with your feelings. You began to slow down, to sit quietly and to look inside.

You may have discovered the value of meditation and everyday mindfulness practices to help you feel calmer, more grounded and more in tune with your intuition. You may also have begun exploring some form of spirituality or faith or started reaching out to others for help, or perhaps you have deepened a connection you already had with yourself or with nature, the Universe or God.

As you have begun to slow down and feel your feelings, you may have become aware of some unhealthy crutches you've been using to sustain you at your current pace or you may have noticed strategies you've developed to stay disconnected from your emotions. Hopefully, you have started to let some of these crutches or coping mechanisms go, or at least you have become willing to do so. Whatever you do, do it when you're ready, in your own time, with gentleness and support.

I wonder if you've noticed any shifts since you began this process. I wonder if any hurt has surfaced or if you're feeling vulnerable. Maybe you're feeling better about yourself than before.

I wonder if the simple act of prioritising yourself and your emotional and spiritual health for a few minutes each day has increased your self-esteem.

If it has, keep going. If it hasn't, persevere. Go deeper. Spend more time looking inside.

Learning to connect to your emotions, meditating and exploring spirituality are all acts of self-care. You're investing in yourself. You are making down payments on a happy, healthy, love-filled future. You are filling up your self-esteem pot.

The importance of healthy self-esteem

Having healthy self-esteem is vital to our ability to form and maintain intimate, loving relationships.

Unfortunately, dating pushes many of our buttons and if we're not adequately prepared, our self-esteem can come under attack. We can be bombarded with questions like: Does he fancy me? Did I talk too much? Does he think I'm too old? Why hasn't she said 'I love you' yet? When will he commit? Is she about to break it off?

In fact, relationships of all kinds are packed with triggers that can undermine our self-confidence if we're not careful.

That's why I'd like to spend some time in this chapter building on the work you did in Step One so you are more equipped to deal with the challenges dating can throw up.

I'd like to invite you to increase your self-esteem further

and to strengthen your emotional core so that you can enter into dating and relationships with strong foundations and feeling good about yourself.

You need healthy self-esteem in order to believe you deserve a lovely partner – someone you're attracted to and with whom you feel safe and loved. If you can believe that, you're more likely to attract somebody who fits the bill.

You also need healthy self-esteem so you can set boundaries with yourself and with the people you date – so you can go home when you want to after a night out or avoid drinking too much and getting closer to a guy than you intended to on a first or second date.

As you form relationships, you need healthy self-esteem to communicate your needs to a partner and to be able to value yourself enough to walk away if it becomes clear your most critical needs are never going to be met. Healthy self-esteem will help you trust that you don't have to stay in a relationship that's harmful, loveless or stagnant. Above all, if you value yourself, you'll feel more resilient and more able to go for what you want in life and in a relationship.

When we ask questions like, 'Does he fancy me?' or, 'Does he think I'm too old?' we are looking for someone else to validate us. We are looking for someone else to affirm our looks or our worth, to tell us that we are attractive and lovable. But if we can do this for ourselves, if we can believe in our own unique beauty and value and if we can esteem ourselves from the inside out, we will be less dependent on external opinions.

This is a good place to be.

One of the mantras that has kept me reasonably sane over recent years is, 'Self-esteem comes from doing estimable things'. The dictionary defines 'estimable' as 'worthy of great respect'.

For me, maintaining a morning routine of meditation, prayer and connection to myself is an estimable act. My day flows much better when I prioritise that routine. If I jump out of bed and race out of the house, something doesn't feel right.

This routine has become a daily act of self-care on a par with cleaning my teeth. If I don't do it, I feel icky, like I've missed out something important.

This is where I'd like you to get to as well. It may not happen overnight, but I hope it happens eventually. That's because I believe that the more we fill ourselves up from the inside, care for ourselves and meet our needs, the more likely we will be to attract suitable partners and form loving relationships.

The danger of being in deficit

Imagine walking into a coffee shop to meet a date when you feel depleted or empty inside. If you turn up with a huge deficit of love and a long list of unmet needs, your date may not go well. Your inner emptiness will be screaming, 'Love me, care for me, respect me, value me, need me, want me, fix me – please!'

If that happens, you could be in trouble. To begin with, you might not get out of the starting blocks with your date. Emotionally healthy men will likely sense there's an empty hole within you, realise it's too deep and wide for them to be able to fill it and walk or run in the opposite direction.

Even if you do succeed in attracting someone, they may be drawn to your vulnerable, needy side, which will leave you open to manipulation, mistreatment or abuse. Or they may have an equally cavernous hole inside them, which might spark fireworks at the beginning, convincing you he must be 'The One'.

When there are bucket loads of chemistry at the outset, it's easy to think, 'This is it. This level of passion reminds me of a Hollywood movie. This is what love is supposed to feel like.'

I know I've thought that in the past.

But in many cases, this intense, fiery connection suggests an unhealthy bond between two people who are too hungry for love and attention for the relationship to survive. They are both so desperate for someone to meet their needs – and so sure they've found their saviour – that they're drawn together like magnets.

If the man or woman is on some form of healing journey, or both are, the couple may be able to understand what's going on, work through the unhealthy side of the attraction and form a stable relationship. If not, it's likely that what began with fireworks will, sooner or later, go up in smoke.

On the other hand, if you're doing your inner work, doing your best to fill the void inside and to give yourself the love, comfort, security, nurturing and care you deserve, you won't be so desperate to receive it from others. You'll have greater self-esteem, be more attractive to healthy partners, feel more certain of what you deserve and be more able to discern if someone is right for you or not.

It took me a long time to come to terms with this but I eventually understood that we can't expect our romantic partners to be everything to us. We can't expect them to fill the gap inside or fix our pain. That's too much responsibility to put on anyone's shoulders. I tried it once and it put such a strain on a relationship that it ultimately broke.

Not long after my dad died, I began dating a man who would be moving to another continent within a few weeks.

Before I go any further, did you spot the two red flags in that sentence? I was grieving the loss of my dad and the guy I fell for was about to leave the country.

Our relationship began in the summer sunshine, with lightness and fun, but as it progressed, heaviness set in.

Some months after my dad's death, I became enmeshed in a difficult, painful situation with my step-mum – we were two grieving women wanting to hold on to parts of the man we'd lost and we weren't seeing eye-to-eye. I needed my partner's support but my need was too great because I'd lost sight of how to support myself. He had become my emotional crutch because I was an emotional wreck.

At the same time, I was beginning to realise how much my Reuters parliamentary job left me feeling dead inside and I was becoming increasingly dissatisfied with London life. I wanted something to change. I wanted to run away and fix my pain.

I stumbled on an answer – a magic bullet. I'd go to the United States and move in with my man. I would try a geographical solution.

We discussed the idea over the phone but he politely and sensibly declined, although that's not how I saw it at the time. He said he'd be happy for me to move to the same town, but I'd have to do so under my own steam. I'd need to find my own place to live and find a job to support myself. Moving in and depending on him wasn't an option.

I felt devastated and rejected. I labelled him a

commitment-phobe and he may well have been, but I now see that I was looking to him to heal my pain and help me find my way out of a very dark place. I was asking too much, more than one person could handle.

I'm not saying it's wrong to reach out to your partner for love and support or to consider giving up your life to make a go of it with him. Love involves risk, after all. But make sure you are making the decision from a place of emotional maturity, not from a place of emptiness. Make sure also that you are supporting yourself as best you can and reaching out to a broader support network. It is unhealthy to put all your dependency needs on a boyfriend or partner.

If you decide to move cities or countries to be with your partner, ask yourself if you are moving for the right reasons, not just because you're lost and you're looking for a quick fix or an escape. If you choose to join your life with somebody else's, it's best to do so feeling as steady, stable and whole as possible.

What does it mean to be whole?
Whenever I talk, blog or write about wholeness, I always come back to the image of an oak tree. I don't claim this metaphor as my own — no doubt I heard it or read it somewhere — but I liked it immediately and I've embraced it body and soul. I've stood on London's Hampstead Heath with my arms around an oak tree and my heart and face pressed against its bark.

Why do I talk about the oak? Well, oak trees are solid, steady and unwavering. They have deep roots that hold them securely in the ground. When they get battered by the elements, they stand firm. They don't fall over in the wind.

Compare that image to a picture of a spindly tree with scrawny branches, shallow roots and a thin trunk. This tree sways back and forth in the wind and it's prone to toppling over when a big gust comes.

Oak trees take a long time to grow strong and tall but that's what we're aiming for. We're aiming for deep roots, a solid core, stability and resilience. We get these things from the inside, by connecting with our feelings, processing them and healing them. We become strong by filling up on self-love, spirituality or faith and by nurturing and nourishing ourselves.

A healthy oak tree is fed and watered. It has all the sunshine and nutrients it needs to maintain its solid trunk, its multitude of branches and its luscious leaves.

This is why self-care is so important on your journey to greater self-esteem. Remember, self-esteem comes from doing estimable things, from caring for yourself, loving yourself and being kind to yourself.

So, is your body or soul craving sunshine or a fresh breeze? Are you eating healthily and giving yourself the nourishment you need? Are you exercising? Are you getting enough rest and play? Are you treating yourself in the way you'd like a partner to treat you or the way you'd treat your child or your best friend? Are you strengthening your core, both emotionally and physically?

A few years back, I took up studio Pilates to try to ease a bad lower back. I used to stand up from my computer after hours of work with a crooked spine and in a lot of pain. I ignored it for as long as I could but finally decided I had to do something about it. I signed up for two 90-minute Pilates sessions per week at great expense, knowing I'd be more likely to keep to my appointments if paying for them had hurt financially.

A year later, I was walking taller, feeling stronger and wearing short skirts for the first time in years. My body changed shape, my posture improved and I felt more confident. Knowing I had a stronger physical core and that I was taking care of myself helped me feel like I had a stronger emotional core too.

Another one of my favourite mantras is, 'We teach people how to treat us'. We do this by the way we treat ourselves. If we're mistreating ourselves by neglecting our needs, punishing ourselves or pushing ourselves too far, others will think it's acceptable to treat us that way too. But if we stand up for ourselves in both our personal and professional relationships and we treat ourselves with respect, others will get the message and follow suit. This goes for our family members, friends, colleagues, dates and partners. And remember, self-respect is an attractive quality.

These days, I try to ask myself a few key questions before I agree to do anything. They are: Is this good for me? Is this in my best interests? Am I cramming too much in? Am I pleasing others rather than taking care of myself?

I then try to pause and reflect before I give an answer. I love the phrase *pause and reflect* as you may have gathered from this book. I repeat it to myself often. Pause and reflect, Katherine. Think about it. Don't rush in.

In the past, I tended to say 'Yes' when I meant 'No' because I was afraid of other people's disapproval or anger. I desperately wanted to be liked. I didn't want others to think I was unhelpful, lazy, selfish or uncommitted. So I would put other people's needs before my own and then end up feeling resentful. I avoided confrontation in the short term but my dishonesty and compliance sometimes damaged the relationship in the long term.

I know many of us are guilty of taking too much on in our careers. But if we say 'Yes' to working through our lunch break or late into the night, our colleagues will get the message they can offload projects on to us and expect them to be finished. However, if we leave the office on time, state clearly that our diaries are full and give accurate estimates of when work will be finished, allowing for sleep, rest and working at a manageable pace, others will begin to respect our boundaries and we will feel better about ourselves.

If we can practise these behaviours in the workplace or in friendships first, we'll find it easier to respect ourselves in our romantic relationships.

Easier said than done, I know, but I'd ask you simply to recognise the importance of estimable acts and self-care to building a healthy, loving relationship with yourself and to understand how important this is for your future.

Pause and reflect

- What estimable acts can you add into your day to feel better about yourself? In what ways can you improve your self-care?
- In your relationships, at home and at work, are you teaching others to treat you well by the way you treat yourself? Is there anything you would like to change? Would you like to stand up for yourself more? Are you prioritising your needs or putting others first?

Listen out for warning bells

I learned about self-care the hard way. In the old days, if I felt tired, I'd feed myself chocolate or drink caffeine-loaded drinks. I used to have a serious Diet Coke habit – sometimes I'd have three a day. Even if my eyes were hurting, I'd force myself to sit for another few hours at the computer because I needed to make sure my work was perfect. If I felt hurt or angry, I'd take myself on a punishing run or do a spinning class at the gym.

I'm still not great at self-care, even after many years of working at it. I've sat too long in front of the computer while writing this book, for example, and I haven't had enough sleep. And I can still resort to chocolate or toast with butter and Marmite when I'm feeling tired or stressed. But these days, I'm aware when I'm pushing myself beyond my limits and I try to stop. I listen out for the warning bells that tell me I'm overdoing it and change my behaviour before I spiral down into a dark hole and feel miserable and depressed.

Those warning bells rang loudly a few years back. I injured my wrist while moving my scooter (I have a pistachio green Vespa) and exacerbated the injury carrying a heavy suitcase on holiday to Spain. While away, I ignored the pain and learned to kite surf, which set me back even further. Coming home, I started to imagine the worst.

I've never been good at being ill or hurt. I have a habit of ignoring the physiotherapy exercises or the doctor's advice, while catastrophising about the life-changing impact of my ailment.

I did that with my wrist. I decided my injury was the end of my writing career as well as everything else I loved, like cycling, swimming and dancing salsa. On top of that, I was in a bad place with my work, doing jobs I really didn't want to do. I was working for myself but I was still accepting projects that put my soul to sleep because I was scared of not having enough money. I knew I was neglecting myself but I carried on regardless.

I was also lonely. I was 43 with no partner and no children. Things looked very bleak and I was crying a lot. One morning, I decided I had reached my limit. I dragged myself to my doctor's surgery and sobbed to my GP. The doctor suggested I needed pharmaceutical help.

The topic of antidepressants had come up on many occasions over the years with doctors, therapists and a psychiatrist I saw after I got signed off work but I had never gone down that route. I know they save lives and help many people get back on their feet and they may have done me good but my personality railed against medication. Taking pills seemed like cheating to me. I liked to do things under my own steam. Plus, I'd spent the previous decade trying to rid my body of artificial chemicals – sugary food, alcohol and so forth – and I was reluctant to pollute it again.

This time, though, I felt I had no choice.

I took half an antidepressant one morning and felt weird. I knew this was part of the process and my body would adjust after a while. I knew I was supposed to sit it out but I didn't like not feeling myself. I took another half a pill the next day and still felt strange.

The following morning, I stopped taking the tablets. Instead, I put the box of antidepressants in my handbag and went for a walk on Hampstead Heath. There, I sat on a log, did some sobbing and had a good think about my life. As I pondered how on earth it had come to this, it became clear to me that I was the source of much of my unhappiness. I insisted on doing work I disliked, I pushed myself to my limits and I had little fun, joy or spontaneity in my life.

I was about to take a pill to help me cope with the dismal existence I had created, but what if I could create a different life? Maybe then I wouldn't need the drugs. I'd got myself into this mess and I was going to try and get myself out of it.

A few days later, I got the chance to prove that I could make myself happy and I jumped at it. I can picture the day clearly. A work meeting got cancelled, the sun was shining and the seaside beckoned. I packed a swimming costume, a sarong and some snacks and then headed for St Pancras Station, en route to Camber Sands on the Sussex coast.

As I moved through the turnstiles and onto the platform, my heart skipped. I felt like a naughty child playing truant from school, only I was an adult, escaping from a life that was boring me to tears and making me depressed.

The day was phenomenal – warm sunshine, blue skies, a secluded spot in the sand dunes, a good book and peace and quiet. I lay there for hours. I wasn't sure if I'd swim but as I walked along the water's edge later in the afternoon, I saw two ladies strip down to their underwear and run in, shrieking, giggling and waving their arms around. That was the impetus I needed. I went in the sea, lay on my back, looked up at the sky and smiled. I felt lucky to be alive.

At the end of the day, I sat on the top deck of the bus back to Rye train station, admired the views and marvelled at the freedom and spontaneity of my seaside trip. When I got back home to my Islington flat, I kicked off my shoes, emptied my wet costume from my bag and watched the sand trickle out.

'You know how to make yourself happy, Katherine,' I said to myself. 'You just need to look after yourself, have fun and give yourself a break.'

If your mood is low or you're bursting into tears every time you go to work, you may need to do something drastic. In your case, this may involve speaking to your doctor about medication, or it may involve practising extreme self-care. It may involve saying 'No' to others so you can say 'Yes' to yourself, or reminding yourself of what's good about life and doing something spontaneous.

Do whatever it takes to get back on track. If you have children, call in a family member or a friend to give you some help. If you work, get signed off sick or award yourself a mental health day or two. Learn to meet your needs, soothe yourself and bring joy back into your life. Once you start, you'll find it gets easier to take care of yourself and fill your life with good things. You'll feel more complete, more confident and more resilient.

That's when you'll be ready to meet your match.

Imagine walking into that coffee shop again to greet your date feeling content, stable and well-nourished like a solid oak tree, instead of miserable, depleted and wobbly. Imagine walking into a party or logging on to a dating website feeling really good about yourself and your life. How would that be? Would it help you to make healthy choices? Would it help you to take risks and be courageous? Would it help you to feel more certain of who you are and what you want?

I believe it would. In fact, I believe it's essential to cultivate your inner oak tree.

You don't need to attain perfect oak status before you date or start a relationship. I've been in a committed relationship with my partner for three-and-a-half years and I still have my spindly tree moments. It's about doing the work, nourishing your core daily, building yourself up from the inside and giving yourself the best possible chance at wholeness so you can form a healthy partnership.

I remember being on a windsurfing holiday with my partner a few years ago and one of the guests asking if I was 'his other half'. I objected and replied, 'We're together, yes, but I'm a whole person in my own right.' I was sort of joking but part of me was serious.

Healthy relationships are formed of two people who are relatively complete or who are committed to doing the inner work it takes to move towards wholeness.

Restore your faith in yourself

Becoming whole is about making our hearts stronger and our lives bigger. To begin this process, write down all the things that make your heart sing then choose one or two of them to do in the coming weeks. Join a choir, a book club or a hiking group. Volunteer at your local charity. Take a cookery or dance class or learn to make cocktails. Go surfing in Cornwall, sign up for a yoga holiday or start saving for that trek to Machu Picchu. Broaden your social networks and deepen your friendships.

Remember who you are. Remember that daring, brave, spontaneous child inside and let her out to play. Remind yourself how strong, courageous, powerful, resourceful and wonderful you are.

We can forget this, can't we? A relationship ends, a boyfriend breaks up with us or nobody contacts us on a dating website and our confidence takes a hit. We stop believing in ourselves.

Worse still, we stop believing we deserve joy, happiness, companionship and love. We retreat. We become smaller and our lives become smaller at the same time.

Do whatever it takes to restore your faith in yourself. Don't expect to feel fearless. Instead, if the fear comes and it takes hold of you, see it as a sign that you're on the right path, that you're challenging yourself and standing up to your inner demons.

If the fear gets too much, seek help. Ask a friend for support, see a therapist or a counsellor or speak to a coach. Then go for it. Don't wait for someone to do it with you. Step out on your own.

Pause and reflect

- Take a moment to reflect on how confident and happy you feel right now. Has your self-esteem been knocked?
- Think about what steps you could take to build or rebuild your self-worth, to make yourself feel happier and whole and to create a more complete life.

Follow your heart

A few years ago, I found myself dreaming of going camping in Spain on my own. All I could think of was taking myself off to Tarifa, a magical village surrounded by white sandy beaches at the southernmost tip of Spain. I'd been there five or six times before when I was dating a man who grew up there but I wanted to go back on my own.

The thought wouldn't go away so I booked some flights and packed my tent. Then the fear set in. What on earth was I doing? Nine days in a tent on my own. What was

I thinking? I'd travelled the world alone in my early twenties but I was younger and braver then, plus I had excess food and alcohol to give me courage. Now it was just me, without my crutches. I was so scared. But I'd paid for the trip so I decided to go.

I needn't have worried. As soon as I landed in Malaga and got into my tiny, white hire car, tuned the radio to Spanish pop and hit the motorway, I knew I'd made the right choice. My heart skipped and I laughed to myself.

Yes, Katherine. Yes.

The holiday was all I wanted it to be. I devoured a few books, slept late in my tent, lay on the beach under a sun umbrella, swam in the sea, ate delicious Spanish food and went dolphin watching in the Strait of Gibraltar. Yes, there were moments of loneliness – those times when I sat eating my evening meal with my book, surrounded by extended Spanish families complete with kids, grandpas, uncles, next-door neighbours and friends. But overall it was fine. I was holidaying with myself and it felt good.

I had listened to my heart, trusted my gut and stepped out of my comfort zone. In doing so, I had restored my faith in myself. I was a multilingual, adventurous, sun-seeking traveller. I had heard the call and I had followed it.

You don't have to go abroad and you don't have to go on your own to feel good about yourself. But tune in to your heart and listen to what it's telling you. Use that voice to guide you towards activities that will help you feel happy and whole.

Think about what steps you could take so you no longer walk around with a void inside that leaves you feeling exposed and vulnerable or that perhaps puts men off having dates with you. How can you become your best friend or your own soulmate? How can you fill your life with wonderful things so you become someone you'd love to hang out with or date? How can you meet your own needs so that you're not desperate for someone else to meet them for you?

Becoming whole is a lifelong journey and I'm not sure we ever get there. But it's amazing to enter into a relationship with a strong sense of self and with a life full of hobbies, activities, friends and future plans. This makes us attractive and it makes for a healthier partnership.

The more complete you feel inside, the better decisions you'll make as you date and enter into relationships. Usually, we're bombarded with choices as we set out on our dating journey, especially in this era of apps and of swiping left or right. There's always a decision to make. Should I text him? Should I send her an email? Should I say I miss him? Should I tell her I love her yet? Should I break things off or give her another chance? Should I commit to him or keep searching for someone else? Should I wear heels or stick with the flats? You know what I mean.

Now, imagine answering those questions with a stronger sense of who you are and with a greater understanding of your worth. How would it feel if you were sure of your value and clear about what you were looking for; if you knew what you were willing to compromise on (or not) and what behaviours were acceptable to you (or not)? Imagine dating with healthy self-esteem, greater confidence and the knowledge that whatever happens, you'll be fine because your inner oak is strong.

Is that an attractive prospect?

This inner strength, this resilience and these high levels of self-esteem are vital pillars of support as you move on to the next step on your journey: identifying your unhealthy patterns.

Step Two: Reflection and action

- Decide on one or two estimable acts you could add into your week.
- Ask yourself if you are teaching your friends, colleagues, dates or partners to treat you with care and respect by the way you are treating yourself.
- Commit to a new act of self-care such as leaving work early, switching your phone off by eight o'clock in the evening or signing up to a Pilates class.
- Think about activities that nourish and nurture your inner oak.
- Before you make a decision, ask if what you are about to do is in your best interests. Is it good for you?

My reflections

Chapter 3

Identify your unhealthy patterns

'Unfinished business doesn't go away. It keeps repeating itself, until it gets our attention, until we feel it, deal with it, and heal'
Melody Beattie

In the previous two chapters, you learned to connect to your feelings, tune in to your intuition, value yourself, strengthen your core and follow your heart. This is essential groundwork for the next stage of the falling in love process: identifying your unhealthy patterns and sorting through your emotional baggage so you can understand what's blocking you from love.

This step on the journey can evoke powerful feelings so make sure you continue to build on your routine of self-care.

If you've been single for a long period or you haven't found love by the time you're in your late thirties, forties or beyond, it's easy to think that you just haven't met him yet.

It's easy to convince yourself that the reason you haven't been attracted to anyone or your relationships haven't worked out is because the right person hasn't come along.

Let me guess, everyone you're attracted to is unavailable for one reason or another. They're either married, partnered up, embroiled in a divorce, wedded to their job, immersed in their religion, addicted to alcohol or drugs, or they live abroad. Either that, or you meet seemingly available single men but you don't fancy them, no matter how much you try. Maybe you don't meet any eligible men at all. Or perhaps the guys you go for are single, but as you get closer, they turn out to be commitment-phobes and they break it off.

If any of this sounds familiar, I have bad news for you – it's not all about the other person. There's a common denominator in all your relationships, all your break-ups and in all those periods of singleness and that common denominator is you.

I spent years pointing the finger at the men I dated (and subsequently broke up with), blaming them because they were afraid of commitment, unfaithful or flaky. I dismissed other guys because they weren't man enough, ambitious enough, sporty enough, or good-looking enough … the list goes on. On the odd occasion, I was given the push or we agreed to part but most of the time it was me who walked away. I thought I had good reason. I thought he was wrong for me. I thought I needed someone different, someone better, someone more …

I'm not saying all my past boyfriends were right for me. I'm just noticing that there was a pattern to my behaviour, a pattern I repeated over and over again. I would leave in search of someone else or dismiss the men I was with as inadequate. I would put the blame at their door, even though it was me who was walking away.

I followed the same pattern with the man I'm in love with now. I broke up with him about three times before I finally came back and we committed to each other. That was three-and-a-half years ago. Each time I walked away, I thought I had good reason and on the surface, maybe I did.

My main objection to him was his objection to parenthood. He didn't want children and I believed I did, or at least I wanted the *chance* to start a family within a loving relationship. Fair enough. But how much did I actually want children and how much was the baby issue a convenient excuse to keep leaving him? Maybe I was using that obstacle to avoid entering into a committed and intimate relationship with all the potential heartache that involved.

On closer inspection, I'd always been ambivalent about motherhood and by the time I got to my early forties, I was beginning to wonder if I'd have the energy to bring kids up. I wondered if I'd end up resenting the loss of freedom and the imposed routines that children inevitably bring.

Besides the children issue, I'd made other decisions about my partner that were instrumental in our break-ups.

Unlike me, he wasn't 'A' type, ambitious or driven. His spelling was poor, he'd studied at Portsmouth Polytechnic and he hadn't had a high-flying career. I'd been to Oxford University and had worked as a globetrotting journalist, hobnobbing with VIPs and sipping champagne in Downing Street. He also had long hair and lived in a tiny bachelor pad with no pictures on the walls – a sure sign of commitment phobia, according to my self-help books. It couldn't possibly work out. Surely I must be able to find a Cambridge man with a six-figure salary, a lovely home and a Ted Baker suit?

Fortunately, throughout our on-off relationship, I was

working with a therapist – an expert in dysfunctional relationships – who was helping me explore my past, dismantle some of my core beliefs and challenge some of the patterns that had either kept me single or had led me in to doomed relationships. He was helping me see the reason why I went for unavailable types and commitment-phobes or why I judged the men I dated as not good enough and went off in search of someone else.

So what was the reason?

It was because I was terrified of commitment myself.

The child inside me equated love and intimacy with hurt and loss so my subconscious mind led me towards men with whom a relationship couldn't possibly work out in a bid to protect me from pain. That's why I chose men who were attached to other women, wedded to their work, addicted to alcohol or even men who turned out to be gay.

Once I understood that and once I identified my unhealthy patterns and sorted through my emotional baggage, I could leave it behind and do things differently.

I believe that, like me, you may struggle to have a healthy, loving, committed and intimate relationship unless you rifle through your baggage and dispose of the unhelpful stuff.

I believe you need to identify the blocks and the behavioural patterns that keep you stuck and challenge any unhelpful beliefs or decisions you've made about yourself and others that prevent you from moving forwards.

Locate your baggage

The best place to start looking for your emotional baggage is in your childhood. Your relationships with your early caregivers and the feelings you had towards them have enormous repercussions for your development and the health of your relationships as an adult. You will have been affected by the way those God-like grown-ups who were in charge of your survival behaved towards you – and each other – as well as any losses or hurts you suffered as a youngster.

I know from experience that thinking about childhood relationships can evoke strong and often confusing feelings, so do seek support or professional help if that happens.

I should point out I'm not a qualified psychotherapist, although I do have a diploma in counselling and psychotherapy skills. I have also experienced more than 10 years of personal therapy and I've been in recovery from addictive behaviours and dysfunctional relationship patterns for more than a decade, so I've learned a lot along the way. On top of that, I've studied scores of self-help books, both as a journalist, a researcher and as an interested party.

My most important qualifications, however, were gained in the school of life, often through painful episodes of trial and error.

I'd like to share some of my experiences and realisations with you in the hope they will help you locate your baggage and identify your blocks. Awareness is the first step to change and my intention is to help you become aware of any potentially unhelpful patterns and core beliefs that may be holding you back. There's no need for you to delve into the darkest regions of your past right now. Simply use this time to reflect on your experiences. Then you can decide whether you want to challenge your patterns and you can explore the most loving way to do that.

As I've mentioned, our relationships with our early caregivers

– with our parents, guardians, teachers, relatives or older siblings – shape the way we relate to others as adults.

So let's start to explore these relationships through the following questions:

1. What was your relationship like with your dad or with the primary male caregiver in your life? Did he die when you were young? Was he always there for you or did he leave and break your heart? Did he stay but was he distant, aloof, absent, busy or short on time? Were you afraid of him? Did he harm you or neglect you in some way? Did you feel you could never please him enough? Did you feel he didn't love you the way you wanted him to? Or was he hugely loving and supportive? Perhaps he was too good to be true? Maybe you put him on a pedestal?

2. And what about your mum? Was she present or absent emotionally? Was she happy or depressed? Was her love wonderful or was it too intense? Did you form the belief that love or intimacy was to be avoided at all costs because it felt suffocating? Could you never please her enough? Was she jealous of your boyfriends or girlfriends? Were you afraid of her? Did she model unhealthy relationship behaviours or positive ones?

3. Did your parents fight or behave in a passive-aggressive way towards each other? Did you come away thinking that if that's what love or marriage looks like, you'd rather give it a wide berth? Or were they so incredibly in love and in tune with each other that their relationship eclipsed all else? Did you feel they'd set a standard you'd never be able to live up to? Were you overly dependent on them, so much so that you never really grew up or

flew the nest? Maybe you're so close to your mum or dad, even now, and so desperate to hold on to that special place in their heart that you're reluctant to form a close relationship with a partner in case that parental love fades.

Pause and reflect

- Take a moment now to think about these questions and any others that come to mind.
- Simply mull them over in your head or jot down some answers in this book or in a notebook if that feels right.
- If feelings come up, allow yourself to feel them. If tears come, let them flow.
- Identify your needs and then do what you can to meet them. Do you need to meditate, write, go for a walk or phone a friend?

Daddy's little girl

When I was in my teens and twenties, I avoided telling my dad about my boyfriends because I wanted to remain his little girl for as long as possible. I thought I could hold on to his love or make him love me more if I didn't grow up.

I remember when I was a sixth-former bumping into my father and step-mum one weekend on Otterspool Promenade, a walkway along the River Mersey near my home in Liverpool. I was with a boyfriend and I cringed. I didn't want Dad to see me with him. I didn't want him to know I was dating at all.

I also recall Dad saying once, 'Katherine isn't interested in boys. She's much more interested in her studies' or words to that effect.

'I get it,' I said to myself. 'My role is to do well at school. That's what Dad wants. That's how to keep his love.'

So that's the decision I made.

If you're a man reading this book, you may sense that your mum would feel hurt or lonely if you decided to move on and commit to a woman, especially if she's on her own, so instead you have flings but never let them develop into anything serious.

The problem is that our subconscious tunes in to the subtle messages we pick up from our caregivers, sometimes misinterpreting them. Or it forms unhelpful beliefs based on our past experiences. It then leads us to act on them. Meanwhile, we simply assume we haven't met the right man or woman yet.

Think about other family members too, brothers or sisters, uncles and aunts, anyone who was significant in your childhood. Even if your family resembles the Waltons, there'll likely be something that impacted the way you relate to others and that contributed to your core beliefs. Even if you think you're baggage-free, you're probably carrying something, even if it's just hand luggage.

To be clear, doing this work isn't about blaming anyone. Your parents did their best with the tools they had at their disposal at the time, and their parents did too. They were the product of their upbringing and perhaps they didn't have it so good. Maybe they weren't given the love, security, nurturing or guidance they deserved or needed in order to develop emotional maturity and pass it on to their children.

Dysfunction of any sort often dates back generations. It's nobody's fault. Therapy wasn't as available or as accepted years ago and self-help books were in short supply. So the purpose of identifying your baggage isn't to point the finger. Your job is simply to understand how your past relationships may be affecting your present ones.

That said, you may feel some anger or resentment and that's perfectly normal. Find healthy ways to deal with it, like talking to a counsellor, therapist, coach or friend. Find a pillow to punch or scribble your angry feelings onto large pieces of paper then tear them up. You could also write a letter to your parents that you don't send.

Better out than in. It's all part of the healing journey.

Understand the push-pull

When I arrived in adulthood, I was well over my baggage allowance and it's taken me a long time to unpack it all. In fact, I'm still coming across some items that have been hidden away in corners. I'll probably be sorting through my baggage for years to come.

But I've done enough unpacking to be able to understand my blocks to love, fall for someone and form a healthy relationship. And I've let go of enough baggage to maintain that relationship, despite a persistent urge to repeat past patterns and self-sabotage.

While each of us has our own story and unique life experience, I know from my friendships and the coaching I've done in this area of love and relationships that some of my patterns resonate with others.

So let me describe a few of my early life experiences and the decisions I made as a result of them, as well as the core beliefs and habits I went on to form.

When my dad sat the eight-year-old me on his knee and told me he was moving out, something went crack inside.

I pushed my head into his neck and sobbed into his shirt. For a little girl who doted on her tall, handsome, entertaining father, the news was devastating.

I also thought I'd done something wrong or that there was something wrong with me. Psychotherapists will tell you it is common for children to react in this way to parental separation or divorce, especially if the adults involved struggle to articulate what's going on or don't manage to reassure the children the split is nothing to do with them.

So my first experience of love really hurt. Love brings loss, I thought, painful, intolerable loss and it must be avoided.

Marriage, from where I was sitting, looked like a bad idea too. It led to arguments, unhappiness and divorce and, for my mum, changeable moods and the burden of bringing up two young children on limited funds. I didn't want to get involved in that kind of thing.

On the other hand, I learned that education and a good career were precious. I decided that doing well at school and in my work was how I was going to please my parents and win their approval and love. Success was also my ticket to a much better life than the one I saw before me.

Can you hear the core beliefs forming in my young brain?

Dad only moved around the corner but that loss, mixed in with other childhood experiences, left a deep, love-shaped hole I was desperate to fill. I've explained how I stuffed the void with sugar and alcohol but I also tried to fill it with male attention and romance to replace what I'd lost.

As a result, I was desperate to be close to a man but as soon as the prospect of emotional intimacy presented itself, I withdrew, pulled back or ran in the opposite direction. I'd come up with seemingly logical reasons why it wouldn't work out and often end it with the classic phrase, 'It's not you, it's me', leaving boyfriends feeling bewildered by my sudden change of heart.

I would pull them in then push them away.

Pull then push.

Pull then push.

(If any men I dated are reading this, I apologise.)

My subconscious would also lead me into relationships with guys who were scared of intimacy themselves – commitment-phobes with their own push-pull routine. I had an uncanny ability to pick them out in a crowd – unavailable men, men with girlfriends or wives, men who were about to move to another continent, men whose work would always come first, men who were so attached to their mothers they couldn't let anyone in or men with untreated addictions. If I kept choosing unavailable types, I could avoid love and protect myself from loss.

I couldn't see this at the time, of course, because passion had taken hold of my senses. I'd feel a magnetic, intoxicating attraction to these men. There was real chemistry and there were often sparks. Surely he must be 'The One'? This intense, dramatic, ferocious love reminded me of the movies. Finally I've cracked it, I thought.

That pull to unavailable types is powerful, isn't it? It's like a drug, and just as difficult to disengage from. It took me years to understand why I felt so drawn to these men – years of repeating the same mistakes and banging my head against the same brick wall.

Eventually, I understood that these men represented my dad. By seeking out relationships with unavailable people, the wounded child inside me was looking for an opportunity to fix her past hurts. She thought she could replay the movie of her childhood but create a different final scene. This time, Dad wouldn't leave or if he did, he'd come back. He'd love her in the way she so desperately wanted to be loved.

This is what is so intoxicating about these relationships. They offer us the opportunity to reverse one of the biggest hurts of our lives – to relive our past and engineer a different, happier outcome. The prospect of pulling this off makes us feel powerful and in control, which is perhaps the opposite of how we felt as children.

This is why some women return over and over again to the same abusive partners or manage to leave one abusive partner only to fall into the arms of another. It's something many of us find incredibly sad to watch and difficult to comprehend, but it's often the result of unresolved pain.

In many cases, these women will have experienced abuse earlier in life so they feel drawn back to it, compelled to repeat it in a desperate attempt to change the ending. The experience of the abuse will also feel familiar and oddly reassuring. It's what they've always known and it's what they believe they deserve. They think it's the best treatment they're going to get.

We may find this kind of behaviour hard to relate to but it's an extreme version of what we do to ourselves when we continually form relationships with unavailable men who can't meet our needs.

I understand these unavailable types can be almost impossible to resist and they find it hard to resist us too. I know because I've been there. But it's likely both parties have identified an opportunity to fix deep wounds – hence the emotional hunger and the fireworks.

If you haven't guessed it by now, I'm passionate about this topic. Sometimes I get angry about it, especially when I hear that a beautiful, intelligent, successful woman has fallen for a man with a girlfriend or wife and has pinned her hopes on him. I get it. I've done it myself. But more often than not, this is a sure-fire way to remain single for many years.

But what about all that chemistry you feel? You've never felt anything like it and you worry you'll never feel anything like it again. He feels it too.

The big problem is that it's not real. It's a fantasy – a Hollywood movie script or a pipe dream. You've got the rush of an illicit or fiery affair, all the passion and the sparks and all the endorphins. Or if your love is unrequited, you're high on a fantasy, floating on a pink cloud, imagining how it would be when you finally got together.

It's perfect. It's ideal.

My therapist introduced me to the work of relationship expert Harville Hendrix, author of *Getting The Love You Want*, who has identified three phases of relationships:

1. The Ideal.
2. The Ordeal.
3. The Real Deal.

This is how I understand the three phases. Unless your internal defence mechanism leads you to find fault with everyone you meet (as mine often did), you'll inevitably experience the Ideal phase with someone, whether the other person is unavailable or not. Without the Ideal phase, you might never get together with anyone. This is the initial period when everything is wonderful. You believe he's perfect for you and your romance feels like a honeymoon. You're high on feel-good hormones. You haven't yet noticed anything about your partner that you don't like.

Then, as you spend more time together and get closer to your partner, you come down off your pink cloud and start to find fault with certain aspects of his looks, behaviour or personality. This is the Ordeal phase. This is the time when you need to negotiate boundaries, manage your differences, speak your truth, ask for your needs to be met and sometimes compromise on your wants, accepting that you live in the real world not in a fantasyland. This requires a good degree of emotional maturity, which is why the first two steps in this book are so important.

This phase can be messy. Your relationship may feel shaky and it may feel that way for a while. You may wonder if it'll stand the test of time. But if you can communicate your needs in a loving way, negotiate healthy boundaries maturely, make some compromises and accept that this tricky phase is an important step on the road to intimacy, you'll come out the other side with a deep connection to your partner and a relationship grounded in reality, truth and trust.

This is the Real Deal.

My therapist suggests an alternative to this third phase and that's No Deal.

In some cases, you'll decide for good reason that you can't manage your differences and that the relationship isn't going to work out. But if you believe in the fantasy of the perfect partner – of an infallible father-like figure who can give you perfect care – you won't be able to make it through the Ordeal phase.

Instead, you'll feel compelled to jump ship as soon as the

Ordeal starts and head off in search of the Ideal again.

The Ordeal phase can feel like hard work. You might think: 'This can't be right. In the movies, relationships look easy – there's passion, hunger, electric sex and relentless excitement. There's none of this walking through treacle stuff. There's no negotiating over money, laundry or whether it's okay to cut your toenails in the bath. I'm out of here. Anyway, that guy over there looks much more suitable. He must be my soulmate.'

And you're off, chasing the Ideal, getting high on the falling in love feeling and floating on the pink cloud. Then the Ordeal kicks in with this new person, you spot someone online who looks more like the Ideal and you bolt – again.

The reason many of us keep searching for the Ideal is because we haven't matured enough emotionally to understand that the perfect partner doesn't exist. We behave in this way because we're afraid of real love and commitment. And we do this because we're disconnected from our feelings and have never learned to process pain or hurt in a healthy way. It feels safer to live in a fantasyland.

But if we want to fall in love, we're going to need to challenge our commitment issues, re-parent ourselves and teach ourselves how to grow up emotionally.

Pause and reflect

- Think about the three phases of a relationship: the Ideal, Ordeal and Real Deal. Can you identify times when you've left a relationship at the Ordeal phase?
- Can you relate to running off in search of the Ideal every time the going gets tough?

- Would you like to change your behaviour and make it through to the Real Deal?
- What support mechanisms would you need in place to do this?

Know when to stay and when to go

Given that many men and women have commitment issues, should you always walk away?

Not always.

Within hours of meeting my partner, I'd identified him as a commitment-phobe. After all, he was a 45-year-old, long-haired singleton who'd never been married, although he'd had several long-term relationships. His mobile phone was pay-as-you-go because he hated being tied in to direct debits or contracts. His home was like a student flat – unloved with a tatty sofa that a friend had donated. Plus, he stubbornly refused to have kids because he didn't want the responsibility or commitment.

At first, I saw an opportunity to change him and the prospect of that was intoxicating. I fantasised that I'd get him to love me with such abandon that he would drop his opposition to fatherhood. Where other women had failed, I would succeed. But he kept saying he couldn't promise he would ever change his mind about kids.

I walked away but I kept going back, all the time berating myself for repeating the behaviours that had kept me single for so long, beating myself up for giving in to the attraction and to instant gratification rather than standing up for my dreams.

When would I ever learn?

But with the help of therapy and the support of friends

who were on a similar journey, I gradually came to understand that I couldn't change my partner and that I had to accept and love him as he was – or not at all. The more I moderated my urge to change him, the more willing he became to commit and as we both let go of a fixed idea of what our future should look like, we allowed ourselves to fall in love.

Now I see how wonderfully matched we are. He is absolutely enough for me. I don't need more or different. He meets my needs for love, emotional and physical intimacy, laughter, safety, security and, God willing, lifelong companionship. I love him so much it brings tears to my eyes.

It's true that when I spend too long on Facebook looking at the picture-perfect lives of friends with kids, I feel sad that I didn't get the chance to have children. There are moments when I question my judgement and doubt my choice, as you will read in my blog post in Appendix I.

Did I, despite all my self-awareness and years of therapy, fall for my dad, who was a father but perhaps a reluctant one? Did I give my heart to someone who couldn't meet my needs? Did I accept less than I deserved? But those doubts are fleeting.

Deep down, I'd always been unsure about motherhood. I also had so much baggage to offload that I didn't fall in love until it was very late in the day to have kids (which is all the more reason for you to do your inner work now if you'd like a biological child). And I'm pleased to say that most of the time, I feel content as a family of two. Being in love like this feels enough of a miracle, given my past.

So back to the question in hand: should you always walk away if he seems unavailable or scared of commitment?

In some cases, the answer is obvious. If he's married or attached to someone else, yes, even if he's promising to leave. I know you don't want to. I know it hurts. I know it's easier to think he'll break it off soon or get divorced. But you deserve better. You deserve someone that's all for you, not just partly for you. And please trust that if it's meant to be, he'll come back to you.

If he's not obviously attached but has fear of commitment written across his forehead, it comes down to your discernment and to all the work you've done on yourself so far.

Try asking yourself the following questions:

1. Have I matured enough and done sufficient personal development work to truly understand that trying to control or change others invariably backfires?
2. Am I sufficiently connected to myself and to my intuition to be able to discern whether this guy has the willingness and the wherewithal to work through his commitment issues and to grow and develop alongside me?
3. Am I emotionally grown-up enough to be able to communicate my needs in a gentle, loving way that won't anger him or prompt him to leave?

You don't need to be perfect or whole for a relationship to work. Far from it, although as you discovered in Chapter 2, the more complete you can become the better. But a relationship can only flourish if both parties are open, honest and willing to do the necessary work to move forwards together. Both of you need to be able to talk through difficulties and manage the Ordeal phase so you can grow, change and develop as a partnership.

Your ability to discern whether a relationship has a good chance of survival will be vastly improved if you've done the work in the previous two chapters. It'll also be vastly improved if you're able to keep your hands off each other for as long as possible.

I've never been great at delaying gratification but over the years I've gained an excellent understanding of the impact getting physical with a guy has on me. I have learned that as soon as I get intimate with a man, it affects my ability to make healthy choices about the relationship, to speak my truth or to make the decision to walk away if that's what I need to do. It's as if a mist descends on me, clouding my senses and impairing my judgement. I can no longer think or behave rationally. I lose the ability to act in my best interests.

So resist the magnetic pull as much as you can. Your heart will thank you for it in the long run.

Pause and reflect

- How strong is your connection to yourself right now?
- Do you feel able to discern whether a relationship is worth pursuing or whether you should declare it a No Deal?
- Can you relate to the idea of a mist descending as soon as you get physical?
- Do you feel able to keep some distance until you're sure of your next steps?

Identify unhelpful beliefs

Part of identifying and understanding your baggage involves digging out any deep-rooted beliefs you hold about love and relationships that are keeping you single.

So, when you think about marriage or parenthood, what comes to mind? Do you envisage some sort of cage or prison cell? Do you feel the weight of responsibility and a huge financial burden? Do you feel suffocated, trapped, quashed or under the thumb? Do you picture monotony, dreariness and a dull routine? Do you see yourself shrinking and your life getting smaller? Or do you imagine a relationship in which one plus one equals three – a partnership that's greater than the sum of its individual parts? Do you imagine your partner adding to your life, your freedom and your joy rather than taking away from it?

What image of relationships did you take away from your childhood? What picture got stamped on your subconscious?

As I've mentioned, I saw strife, disunity, separation and unhappiness. I sensed that my mum's freedom and dreams had been curtailed. I felt the burden of financial woes. In comparison, university, world travel, career and financial independence won hands down. Somewhere along the line, I must have decided that I couldn't have all those things and love and family as well. I must have thought I had to choose between them. I see things differently now.

While we're on the topic of core beliefs, can I invite you to identify any decisions you've made about yourself that may be holding you back and blocking you from having a healthy relationship? If you're still doing the work from Chapter 2, you'll be feeling a lot better about yourself by now. You'll be doing estimable acts, teaching people how to treat you, loving and nurturing yourself and raising your self-esteem.

One factor you need to be aware of, particularly as you age and especially if you haven't had children but still want them, is that you can start to get down on yourself.

'I'm over the hill. Nobody's going to want me. He's going to prefer a younger model. I'm too fat, too set in my ways, too grey, too infertile, too controlling, too …' Fill in the blanks.

What script have you written for yourself? What story are you telling yourself? Maybe you feel you have good reason to think that way. Perhaps you've been rejected a few times. Perhaps you've been traded in for a woman 10 years younger than you or overlooked on dating websites because of your age. It could be that the only men who contact you online are several decades older than you, already drawing their pension. If so, it's no wonder you're down on yourself. It's not surprising that you've lost hope.

But I truly believe that there's someone for everyone if we want to be in a relationship, provided we understand that we're not going to attract love into our lives if we continue to feed our minds with negative thoughts. We're not going to draw positive, healthy men towards us if our vibe screams doom and gloom.

I'm not telling you to cheer up or to pull yourself together. That wouldn't be loving. That's not how I operate. But I'm hoping by this stage on your journey you'll have done some essential healing. You'll have shed some tears, let go of some baggage and you'll be feeling ready to step out with a new mindset.

For now, though, let's focus on identifying any core beliefs and any unhealthy patterns that might be keeping you single.

Over to you

First, take some time out to do some meditation. Ideally, do it for a longer stretch of around 30 minutes. The best time for this may be at the weekend or on a day when you can carve out some space. Afterwards, find a large pad of paper (I prefer A3) and do some drawing or take out a journal and write freely. What core beliefs do you hold about yourself and about relationships? Write them down. Get them all out on paper.

Next, spend some time looking back over your romantic history. Think about and write down the relationships you've had. Include everything from casual liaisons to long-term relationships to marriages. Make sure you list all your significant others as well as the not-so-significant ones.

Now, can you discern a pattern in your relationships? Are you always attracted to the same types? Do all the people you date turn out to be afraid of commitment? Are they emotionally, physically, spiritually or geographically unavailable? Do you go for men who are unfaithful, abusive, needy or suffocating?

What about the people you could have gone out with but didn't fancy? Do you find it impossible to feel attracted to good, reliable men or women? Are you always the one who instigates the break-up or does the other person walk away from you? Are there always fireworks at the start but then the relationship fizzles out?

Whatever you notice, write it down.

You may not want do this work all in one go and it's fine to take several days or weeks. On the other hand, you may not need a lot of time to see your patterns. You may take one look at your romantic history and instantly see there's an undeniable thread running through all your relationships.

Once you've done this exercise, spend some time making connections or parallels between the men you've had relationships with and any childhood experiences or figures from your past. Do the people you go for resemble your father, brother or another male caregiver in the way they look, act or treat you? If your dad was absent, distant or unreliable, can you see those qualities in the men you're attracted to? What about your mum? Can you identify some of her qualities in the partners you choose? Or do you go for people who are the exact opposite of your parents?

Could it be you're trying to rewrite your past, only with a different outcome? Are you trying to fix old wounds? Are you running away from intimacy or love or keeping men at arm's length because you're scared of loss? Could it be you're subconsciously picking commitment-phobes because you're terrified of falling in love and (potentially) getting hurt? Are you dismissing good men because you fear commitment and you're unwilling to risk your heart?

I don't mean to scare you with these questions or send you running off to see a therapist (although that's a path I decided to take and I'm delighted I did). My intention is to encourage you to take a gentle inventory of your love life and your core beliefs, so you're more aware of your patterns, your baggage and your blocks.

While you're going through this process of inner investigation, make sure you take good care of yourself by getting plenty of rest, spending time in nature, soaking in long baths, putting yourself first and doing estimable acts. This is important work and it's going to take it out of you so make sure you're filling yourself back up again. And keep working on that connection to yourself, to your intuition and, if you choose, to a power greater than yourself. Keep strengthening your inner oak.

You're going to need a strong connection to your intuition, sound discernment and lots of inner strength and resilience to take the next step on the journey: to overturn your negative beliefs and challenge your unhealthy patterns of behaviour. We'll begin that process in the next chapter.

Step Three: Reflection and action

- Begin to recognise the impact your early life experiences had on your adult relationships.
- Explore the core beliefs you formed about yourself and about commitment or marriage.
- Take an inventory of any past relationships and look out for recurring patterns.
- Keep loving and nurturing yourself and connecting to your feelings.
- Seek professional help if the feelings are overwhelming.

My reflections

Chapter 4
Do things differently

'Two roads diverged in a wood, and I –
I took the one less traveled by,
And that has made all the difference'
Robert Frost

In the previous step, you identified your unhealthy patterns, located your baggage and got in touch with any unhelpful beliefs that may be standing in the way of love. Now it's time to change those patterns, unpack your baggage and undo your negative core beliefs. It's time to remove your blocks.

This is game-changing work, life-changing even, but it's challenging too so it can't be done overnight. Unpacking your baggage is like peeling an onion. There are many layers to get through. The outer ones may come off easily, sometimes completely intact. The inner layers may stick to the ones underneath so they tear and come off in strips. Your eyes may sting and they'll probably water. So go gently. Don't rush. Be kind to yourself. If it does hurt, remember that these are growing pains, a necessary step on the journey to emotional maturity, self-awareness, self-love and true partnership.

Some people are lucky. They got to do their growing up at the appropriate time – in their childhood, teens and twenties. They emerged from their youth with healthy self-esteem and a good understanding of personal boundaries. In other words, they learned how to set limits for themselves and how to set them with others. They arrived in adulthood with minimal obstacles to love and both the desire and the ability to form committed relationships.

I don't know about you but I spent many single years looking at these people with bemusement. They seemed to travel through life's various stages with relative ease – from career to marriage to children, then a job change, a move to the coast, retirement and grandkids.

Now, I'm well aware of the folly of judging people's insides from their outsides – I know Facebook only shows us photographs of shiny, happy, trouble-free people. But there are those who seem to take to relationships naturally while others watch from the sidelines, wondering what on earth is wrong with them and why their love life looks like a car crash. They can't fathom why they struggle to find anyone to go out with or why all their relationships fail.

I stood on the sidelines for a long time and I put this down to not maturing when I was supposed to. The compulsive behaviours I turned to as a young woman around food, alcohol and relationships with men disconnected me from my feelings. They also stunted my emotional growth, so much so that when I eventually stopped binge eating and binge drinking in my thirties, I felt like a child in a scary, grown-up world. I felt afraid, insecure and clueless about how to navigate life and relationships without my crutches. Like a baby learning to walk, I kept bumping into obstacles, falling down, getting bruised and bawling my eyes out. Slowly, though, I found my way.

I learned to nurture and parent myself so I could meet my needs and become my own best friend. I learned to soothe myself in healthy, rather than addictive, harmful ways. I learned to speak my truth and to navigate relationships without getting too hurt or hurting others too much. Ultimately, I developed enough inner strength to be able to take the risk of giving my heart to another, knowing I'd survive even if it didn't work out.

I was 43 by that point. So it's never too late, provided we're courageous enough to face whatever it is that's blocking us.

Expecting a different future

There are two strands to your work in this step – one involves thoughts, the other involves actions. Let's start with your thoughts.

In the previous chapter, we explored the beliefs we hold about ourselves and about relationships. We identified the negative things we say to ourselves as well as any unhelpful images we associate with long-term relationships, commitment or marriage.

As I've said, awareness is key to change, so we're halfway there. We now need to unpick those beliefs and learn to believe the opposite.

Affirmations are a great place to start. We can begin affirming positive things about ourselves, about the way we look, how attractive we are, both inside and out, how intelligent we are or how generous, kind or loyal we are. If the idea of doing this makes you cringe and you're on the verge of throwing this book out of the window, bear with me. I'm pretty sure, if you're really honest with yourself, you can find some aspects of yourself that you love or at least like. If not, you may need to go back and repeat Steps One and Two so you can establish a kinder, more loving and more nurturing relationship with yourself.

Remember, negative self-talk is a convenient defence mechanism – it means you don't have to get out there and try to find someone to date. If you keep running that negative script in your head, you'll stay stuck.

So try to affirm the opposite of your negative beliefs. You don't have to go over the top and declare you look like Cindy Crawford or say you're the most eligible single woman in town. You just have to do enough to counter any unhelpful messages that might be squatting in your head. For example, you could say: 'I'm a loving, caring person who'd make a great partner'; 'I'm a good person'; 'I have a good heart'; 'I'm fun to be with'; or, 'I have an adventurous spirit'.

As you do this, try to remember we are all wonderfully, beautifully unique.

If you're struggling to come up with something, ask close friends or family members you trust for their opinion of you, or simply look for evidence to counter your negative beliefs. Do you have a large circle of friends? Are people naturally drawn to you? Are you often asked to lead a team? Do people show up for you when you need them? Find real-life proof to silence the voices in your head.

If affirmations don't work for you, don't worry about it. I've used them at certain times in my life but I don't use them all the time. I often call on them in moments of crisis, like when I'm about to have a conversation in which I need to stand up for myself, something I find excruciating but that

I'm getting better at. I say things like, 'I have a right to ask for what I want' or, 'I deserve to get my needs met'. I usually feel stronger afterwards.

You can also do something to counter your negative beliefs. If you're feeling unattractive, try to make yourself feel more attractive – dress differently, get your hair cut, go for a massage, take a spa day, have a bath or moisturise your skin. Find ways to give yourself a treat to boost your spirits. Buy yourself a gift. Go to the movies one afternoon when you're supposed to be at work (that always does it for me. It feels so decadent, particularly for a workaholic perfectionist) or take a trip down the River Thames with the tourists. Whatever floats your boat.

Similarly, you need to counter any negative core beliefs you have about men or women and relationships. If you believe all men are unreliable or untrustworthy, look for evidence in your life (or in the lives of your friends and family) that proves the opposite. Notice the good guys more often rather than focusing on the ones who've let you down. And if you think marriage or committed relationships are boring and monotonous – something akin to a prison sentence – look for couples who are doing life differently. Maybe they're sailing around the world with their kids or driving across America in a beat-up Cadillac. Maybe they're fulfilling their dreams, both individual ones and shared goals. Look for the positives in the partnerships around you. I couldn't see many before, but now I know they are there.

One tool that can help you create more positive beliefs about yourself, your relationships and your future is a vision board. You can use vision boards to map out your dreams and design the future you aspire to have.

This can be as simple as taking a large piece of paper and drawing pictures of things you'd love to have in your life in the not-so-distant future or writing down words. I have lots of these pictures from over the years. Pretty much all of them feature the sea (I'm now living at the beach) and words like *adventure*, *travel*, *love*, *sex*, *partnership* and *fulfilling work* (much of that has come true too).

Alternatively, if you're feeling creative, get a stack of magazines and spend a few hours flicking through them. Cut out images and words that jump out at you and then stick them onto a piece of paper or into a booklet.

I first did this about seven years ago, when I went on an inspirational trip to Mozambique with a group of women and a wonderful charity called 'Could You?' I still have the vision booklet I made. Again, there are images of the sea, of a woman cycling in the countryside and of a couple entwined. All that has come true. There's a dog (my partner and I might get one soon), a diamond ring (which I'll have as soon as I make up my mind and choose one) and a woman swinging a child around by the seashore (I don't have a child of my own but I have three nephews and a goddaughter who can come and stay with me at the beach).

There are also words like *blogging* (I blog regularly and it's been a lifesaver), *TED* (I hope to do a TED talk sooner or later) and the phrase *our story begins every morning* (because I believe it does). I've kept my vision booklet ever since and I look at it quite often. In fact, I can see it from here, resting at the bottom of a noticeboard in my office in the home I share with my partner not far from the sea.

So try to envisage a happier future, one in which you are in a healthy, loving relationship. Imagine the joy of being in love and sharing your life with someone, of planning adventures in a partnership. Imagine it and hold on to that feeling of excitement and anticipation. Expect things to change. Believe your life will be different in a year from now.

If this feels false, if a negative cloud is hanging over you, try doing what you can to get out from under it. Try writing a gratitude list or going for a walk in the sun. When things get really bad for me, I go in the sea, whatever the weather. It never fails to change my mindset.

Pause and reflect

- Which one of these exercises would you like to try? Would you like to write some affirmations to counter your negative beliefs, or would you like to create a vision board of your future?
- If you're ready, begin that now or find a different exercise that resonates with you.

Changing your behaviour

Let's now look at your actions.

As you begin to believe you deserve a brighter future, you will find it easier to change the patterns in your relationships and to behave differently to how you've always behaved, both on dates and in a partnership.

One tool that will help is the practice of pausing and reflecting before making a decision, which we discussed in Chapter 2. This will help you to slow down, connect to your feelings and act in your best interests.

When out on a date or when negotiating boundaries in a relationship, check in with your intuition (you should be getting good at this by now!) and try asking yourself the following three questions:

1. What would I normally do in this situation?
2. How has that worked out for me in the past?
3. How would it feel to try something different this time?

If your pattern is to fall for unavailable men, resist sending a message to the bloke in Berlin if you live in Birmingham (unless it's clear he's heading your way soon, and not just for a weekend).

I'm not saying long-distance relationships can't work out. You probably know a woman from Birmingham who's married to a guy from Berlin whom she met online. It happens. If two people are committed enough to making a relationship work, they'll make it work. I was living in London when I fell for my partner who was in Dorset, although I had plans to move to the coast and Poole seemed a great place to live, as a single woman or in a relationship. But if you have an undeniable pattern of falling for men who live far away, be aware that your subconscious could be running the show. Understand that your wounded inner child could be leading you to unavailable men to keep you safe from intimacy and protect you from hurt. And remember, unavailability comes in all shapes and sizes – emotional, physical, geographical, intellectual, spiritual and so forth.

Similarly, if a guy tells you early on in your courtship that he still lives with his ex-wife or that his ex-girlfriend won't leave him alone, seriously consider walking away until you're sure he's managed to cut ties with his past love. You may well be drawn to him. You may feel that magnetic, irresistible pull. You may desperately want to believe him when he says it's all over, that she's moving out next week or that he'll delete her number from his phone. But take a moment to ask yourself whether this scenario feels familiar.

Have I been here before? Does this person or situation remind me of someone or something from my recent or distant past? Is this relationship truly going to meet my needs? Do I really want to invest my time and energy here? Is this good for me?

Be honest with yourself. Sit with yourself for as long as it takes to hear your intuition. Do you feel peaceful at the prospect of moving forward with this person or do you feel anxious and uneasy? Once you have your answer, muster up as much courage as you can and speak your truth. Say what you're willing to accept and what you're not. Set some boundaries. Stick to them. And, if necessary, walk away.

Turning my own ship around

It's taken me years to change some of my unhealthy relationship patterns and it's been a painful process at times, requiring me to dig very deep and to tap into a well of courage I didn't know I had.

In my twenties and early thirties, when my compulsive, self-harming behaviours were at their height, I did things I'm not proud of but for which I now forgive myself. I've come to understand that a hurt, confused child was in my driving seat, desperately seeking love, seeking someone like my dad so she could recreate her past and engineer a happy ending.

I was incredibly attracted to distant and unavailable men: men in marriages or committed relationships, emotionally unavailable men, men on other continents and men who were gay – perhaps the ultimate form of unavailability.

I remember being infatuated with a guy who had a long-term girlfriend. He gave the impression he wasn't hugely happy in that relationship and that it might end at some point. Nevertheless, he was taken. We had a fling, facilitated by too much wine. After that, we struck up an email relationship since we lived several hundred miles apart.

I remember the buzz I used to get from checking my inbox and seeing his name there – a *frisson*, a feeling of being desired, of something illicit and therefore exciting that brightened an otherwise dull work day and momentarily boosted my self-esteem. Eventually, I realised the error of my ways and found the courage to break it off. Deep down, I knew it wasn't good for me. I knew I was harming myself, and harming others too. I asked him not to contact me and went cold turkey. It was like coming off a drug.

Then, when I finally felt I was over him, when my love hormones had subsided and the fantasy image of our 'happily ever after' was no longer quite so vivid, I got back together with him. Yes, you heard me right. I went through the pain of withdrawal and extricated myself from the relationship, only to start it up again. It was a brief encounter. I came to my senses quickly, broke it off and went cold turkey once more.

Looking back, it seems like madness, like banging my head against a brick wall or ripping off a plaster on a particularly hairy part of my arm, sticking it back on, then tearing it off again.

'Insanity is doing the same thing over and over again and expecting different results', Albert Einstein is believed to have said (although the origin of this famous quote is disputed).

I fitted the definition perfectly. I harmed and sabotaged myself repeatedly in relationships. Finally, though, I learned to love myself enough to want to change and I found the courage to ask for help.

Therapy, meditation and the companionship of others who shared my self-sabotaging patterns and who were also trying to change helped me break a cycle that had been a major factor in my singleness. Slowly, I developed a new muscle – the ability to act in my best interests and put my wellbeing first.

My progress wasn't without relapse. I remember returning home late at night on the Stansted Express after a disastrous weekend in Ireland with a guy I'd met in a London club a few weeks before. I'd invested a lot in that weekend and had high hopes for a relationship with a man I found attractive. I'd booked a luxurious hotel room for us with a sunken bath.

After a few drinks with his friends, I thought we'd head back for some romantic time alone. Instead, he popped some mind-altering pills with a mate and then insisted on going to another nightclub. I didn't know how to say 'No'. By the time we got back to our room, we were on different wavelengths, different planets even. I felt lonely and worthless, but I still went to bed with him. I can see myself now, crumpled up on the train back from Stansted, my head against the window and a lump in my throat. It hurts.

Victories, big and small
So there were setbacks but as I grew stronger, there were victories too, including one vivid memory from a few years

ago. I was in my early forties when my hairdresser persuaded me to try the dating phenomenon that was Tinder. I didn't hold out much hope. I thought it was just for hook-ups and I'd learned my lesson about brief encounters by then. But I was getting nowhere on the standard dating sites so I decided to give it a go.

I connected quite quickly with an intelligent, good-looking man who was a few years younger than me. There was chemistry, a magnetic pull, but I was aware of my tendency to throw myself into a relationship before ascertaining who the guy was, so I summoned all my strength and exercised physical restraint.

Plus, something didn't feel right. He seemed reluctant to choose where we should meet or what we should do on our dates. Arrangements came down to me and they often happened at the last minute because I was waiting for him to step up to the plate.

I didn't expect my date to always book the restaurant or choose the movie every time we went out. I was happy to do my share of the decision-making, even if decisions weren't my strong point. I'd also learned by then to give men the benefit of the doubt. If they lacked confidence or self-esteem, I could now give them a break, whereas in the past I'd have judged them as weak and marched off. I'd realised we were all human, just doing our best.

But even with my newly open mind, something was niggling away at me. He would cut dates short and wasn't available much at weekends. It was hard to pin him down and there was a distance between us.

By this stage in my life, I was ready for a proper relationship. I wanted a partnership of the 'two feet in' kind, but I was beginning to wonder if Tinder guy and I were on the same page. He didn't seem willing to do much more than get his big toe wet. It was bothering me.

In the past, I would have ignored that tap on my shoulder and that uneasy feeling in my gut. I would have taken whatever he was offering and hurled myself into the relationship with little regard for my delicate heart. I would have got physical and allowed my judgement to be clouded by the mist that descended upon me as soon as I took my clothes off. But I'd come far. I'd gone through the process of 'making the same mistakes and expecting different results' enough times to know that the outcome would always be the same. I was over 40. It was time to behave differently.

I bit the bullet one Saturday afternoon when we were cuddling on the sofa in my flat. I detached my lips from his, unravelled myself from his arms and looked him in the eye. I knew what I was going to say. I'd written it down and practised my lines over the phone with friends.

I told him what I was looking for. I told him that I wanted to be in a committed relationship with someone. I said I wanted to spend time with my boyfriend, go on weekend breaks with him and, if all went well, move towards a partnership.

I said it would be good to know what he was looking for, to know if he was on the same page as me or if he was looking for something different. I told him I didn't need an answer immediately. He could go away and think about it. No pressure. But I would like to know his thoughts when he felt ready.

He listened solemnly as I spoke my truth, thanked me for my honesty and said he'd think about my question and get back to me. It wasn't as hard as I'd imagined. He didn't freak out. In fact, it brought us closer, which wasn't hugely helpful because it was getting late and he was in danger of missing his last train home.

We resumed kissing and I could feel myself hovering on the edge of the danger zone. It was dark outside, our chemistry was doing its thing and my bedroom was just steps away. The thought of delaying gratification seemed so dull compared with the alternative. But something – the weight of experience, a compendium of past heartaches, a new maturity and a growing sense of self-worth – stopped me. I hurried him out of the house to the station.

Amazing. One small step for womankind but one absolutely ginormous step for Katherine. I'd broken the cycle, stood up for myself and acted in my best interests. I'd turned my ship around. I felt elated, over the moon and delighted with how far I'd come.

Over the next few days, I did my best to stay calm, to wait patiently for his response and to avoid putting pressure on him. A few weeks later, he gave me his answer. He liked me and he wished he were in a different place but he wasn't there yet. He wasn't ready to consider a committed relationship.

I felt sad and disappointed but incredibly proud of myself. I hadn't got the outcome I'd wanted but this felt like a breakthrough. I had saved myself heartache and pain. I had kept the dreaded mist at bay and honoured my dreams.

Soon after, though, self-doubt kicked in. I'd spoken too soon. I'd hurried him. I should have let things develop a bit more. I'd come over all heavy when I should have kept things light. I'd sabotaged my chances of a potentially great relationship with a guy I really liked. Was it too late to go back, to tell him not to worry, to say we could go at his pace?

I was obsessed with him for a while, with our fantasy future and with what I deemed to be the huge mistake of speaking my truth. But as I put some distance between us and refrained from contacting him, the obsession subsided and I saw our conversation for the huge achievement it was. I had faced my fears, risked loss, experienced rejection and come out of it with my heart reasonably intact, my head held high and feeling good about myself.

I'd created a new memory, one that could help counter all the painful ones from my past. It was a memory I knew I could draw on the next time I had an opportunity either to do as I'd always done or to take the road less travelled.

If I hadn't made the decision to stand up for my dreams, I could have spent that night with him. Maybe I could have done so anyway, even knowing the relationship was about to end. Perhaps that's what you'd have done and maybe you'd have been fine. I used to think I could spend the night with a guy and never see him again without feeling hurt. I used to think my attitude to brief encounters was similar to what you'd traditionally expect of a man. I prided myself on my nonchalance. I felt chuffed when a male friend said I was more like a bloke than a woman when it came to flings.

That's the level of denial I was in. That's how convincing my mask used to be. That's how numb I was to my feelings and how detached I was from my true self.

As it turns out, I'm one of the most emotionally sensitive people I know. I'd call myself a Highly Sensitive Person or HSP. I'm easily hurt, I cry at the slightest of things and I'm incredibly affected by my environment. I'm pretty delicate, in fact (even if I am becoming more resilient). But being vulnerable felt frightenting so I pretended to be the opposite for years. It felt much safer that way.

Pause and reflect

- I wonder if my story rings any bells. Have a think about whether you have repeated the same mistakes and expected different results in your relationships. Have you returned to partners despite knowing they weren't good for you? Have you disguised your true feelings, from yourself and from others?
- Close your eyes for a moment and get in touch with your emotions. You may feel sad about the way you have treated yourself or allowed others to treat you. Feeling the feelings is an important part of the healing process.

Know your limits

Each of us needs to define our limits: the behaviours we can cope with and the ones that bring us too much pain. Your limits will depend on your age, your life stage, how sensitive you are and how far along you are on your journey. The important thing is to develop self-awareness and to notice your patterns, even if you're not ready to change them yet. Be aware of how you feel. Do you still feel compelled to repeat your old behaviours or do you want to try and change? If you want things to be different, you deserve to open your eyes and see how they are right now.

If you do want to experiment with doing things differently, make sure you get some support. Find someone who can help you with accountability and who can remind you of the loving commitment you've made to yourself. Find someone who's aware of your past patterns and how much heartache your behaviours have caused, someone who's on your side. Speak to a counsellor, to a friend who's on the same path or find a community of people who are engaged in personal development or who are on a journey of spirituality or faith. Join one of my groups if you would like to. You will find details at the end of this book.

There's something incredibly powerful about being seen and heard. Sharing our truth with others and allowing ourselves to cry on someone else's shoulder moves us more than crying alone. At least this is my experience.

I've done a lot of crying, both on my own and in company, and the latter is always more healing. And although I've been on this journey for a long time, I make sure I'm always supported. My internal support network is much stronger and more effective now than it used to be, so that helps me manage my emotions. I use tools like meditation, prayer, journaling and so forth most days. But I also see a therapist and regularly meet and speak with fellows and friends who are on a similar journey of transformation and self-discovery.

If you have setbacks, do not fret or beat yourself up. It may feel like you're taking two steps forward and one step back at times, but you're moving in the right direction. By doing this work, you're exercising a neglected muscle and building a new inner strength that you can draw on every time you're faced with a choice. So don't kick yourself when you're down – love yourself even more.

If all this feels like too much hard work or if you feel this introspection, self-analysis and navel-gazing is dragging you down, don't worry. It's only this intense for a limited period of time. While doing this work, you may feel as if you've lost your va-va-voom, that you're not the bubbly, fun, optimistic person you used to be. But keep going. I promise you'll get your sparkle back at a later stage in the journey. I certainly did. Also, remember to balance this deep, inner work with some light-hearted activities and acts of self-love.

Most importantly, keep moving forwards. Keep growing in self-awareness. Keep on trusting the process. I promise you'll reap the benefits.

Once you've identified and begun to challenge your patterns and remove your emotional blocks to love, you'll be ready to break any ties with lost loves and to clear the decks to make way for a new way of being and a new relationship.

That's what we'll be doing next.

Step Four: Reflection and action

- Think about the best way to counter your negative beliefs, perhaps through affirmations or by creating a vision board.
- Decide which patterns and behaviours you'd like to change and put some support mechanisms in place to help you.
- Make a note every time you change a pattern or do something differently, no matter how small, and celebrate your achievement in some way.
- Keep loving and nurturing yourself and connecting to your feelings.
- Before you pursue a relationship, pause and reflect and ask yourself if you've been here before. How did it work out last time? Would you be willing to try a different path?

My reflections

Chapter 5

Let go of lost loves

'Sometimes we stare so long at a door that is closing that we
see too late the one that is open'
Alexander Graham Bell

Over the course of the last four chapters, you explored
ways to connect with yourself, develop your inner resources
and increase your sense of self-worth. You also identified
unhelpful patterns in your relationships and unearthed
negative core beliefs. Most importantly, you began to
challenge your self-sabotaging patterns, undo your harmful
beliefs and remove your blocks to love.

One pattern you may have noticed when you explored
your romantic history is that you have a tendency to hold
on to relationships from your past. It's tempting to keep
a flame burning for an old love or to stay in touch with
ex-boyfriends, checking in now and then by text or email
or keeping track of them on Facebook. Or perhaps you
and your ex are now 'friends with benefits', two people who
engage in familiar and comfortable sex every now and then,
no-strings attached.

What could possibly be wrong with that if there's nobody

else on the scene? Nobody's getting hurt and you can call it off when you meet someone else, right?

I understand the desire to have somebody there, even if you know the relationship will never work out. It makes you feel attractive, desired, safe and less alone. Those brief encounters meet both a physical and an emotional need. But while the short-term benefits are obvious because you get instant gratification and a connection that's free of the messiness of a committed relationship, I'm afraid you might be shooting yourself in the foot in the long term.

Keeping a past liaison on the back burner can reduce or even ruin your chances of finding a partner with whom you can form a lasting relationship.

That's why the fifth step is about letting go of lost loves and clearing the decks so that you are ready for something much better.

The problem with having companionship or sex on tap is that you get little opportunity to build up your inner resources. You don't learn to soothe yourself in healthy ways or experience all of your feelings – both essential steps on the journey to maturity and a loving relationship. If you miss out these steps, you're likely to end up with rocky foundations.

We've established that it's good to ask for help, but make sure you look for support in the right places, not with people with whom there's the possibility of intrigue or sex. Seek comfort, love and companionship from those who have your best interests at heart.

Inevitably, you'll know people who didn't let go of lost loves or clear the decks but who ended up in a seemingly happy relationship. You'll know men or women who haven't had a period of singleness or experienced being on their own in their entire adult lives. You may know people who met their wife or husband while still entangled with an ex and who managed to cut the old ties instantly and embrace a new life with no negative repercussions at all.

It's worked out for them and that's fair enough.

But I'm not writing this book for them. I'm writing it for you – for the person who's single and doesn't want to be, whose habitual way of doing things hasn't, as yet, produced the desired results.

So if you are hanging on to old relationships and you're using past loves as a crutch, a fix or a pick-me-up, I'd like to invite you to do two things.

Firstly, look at these relationships and ask yourself how they're serving you. Understand what you get from them – is it affection, a self-esteem boost, a pressure release or something else?

Secondly, if you conclude that these relationships are not good for you in the long run and that they're getting in the way of you being open to someone else, find the courage to distance yourself from them, even if it's just for a little while. I believe it's difficult to open our hearts to a new partner if an old one is still hanging around, particularly if we're sensitive people. So try letting go of the ex to free up a bit of space.

You don't need to fall out with past loves. Perhaps you can explain that you're taking some time for yourself and you won't be in contact for a few weeks or even several months. That means no calls, texts, coffee meet-ups, dinner dates or late night visits for a while.

Personally, I'm a fan of cutting off all contact for a period because I know I can't entirely trust myself – I have an addictive personality and limited willpower. I struggle to act in my best interests. You may not need to go to such extreme lengths. You may be better at holding your boundaries and being in touch without being tempted to meet up. By this stage on your journey, you should have a better sense of self, a more accurate gauge of what you can cope with and a good idea of your limits. But don't underestimate the pull of comfort, physical intimacy or sex, and don't overestimate your inner resolve.

Pause and reflect

- Is there someone from your past you need to break ties with, even just for a while?
- Are your encounters with an ex taking up valuable time and preventing you from being fully open to meeting someone else?
- Do you feel ready and willing to let go of lost loves?

Making space in your head

It's important to remember that not all unhelpful relationships are physical ones. We may have a lost love whom we no longer see but who's taken up permanent residence in our head. Every time we meet someone new, we compare him to the one who got away and the new guy never matches up. We fantasise about what could have been, imagining a perfect union that's free from the stresses and strains of real-life relationships. We need to break these mental bonds as much as we need to let go of the physical ones.

As you pull away, prepare yourself to feel some withdrawal and some loss. Even if there were no strings attached in terms of long-term expectations, there'll still be ties that have to be cut. Even if the relationship was make-believe, it'll hurt to watch your cherished fantasy collapse. You may hit the ground with a thump. This is a time for extreme self-care – long baths with bubbles and candles, slow walks in nature, meditation, journaling, yoga or whatever you've found that soothes you and helps you to feel supported and held in a safe space.

Whatever you were getting from the relationship or the fantasy, you now need to give this to yourself – love, approval, connection, security, warmth or, dare I say it, orgasms. Then, once you've wrapped yourself for long enough in a giant comfort blanket of your choice, you'll begin to heal and feel ready to face the world.

As you emerge from your cocoon, try doing some gentle exercise – something like Pilates to strengthen your core or some slow yoga. This will allow you to get into your body and out of your head. It will help you to improve your posture, stand taller, and feel better about yourself. Or maybe get your hair cut, buy a new dress or go on a spa weekend with friends. Fill yourself up and feed your inner oak. Throughout this period of healing and restoration, you may have your wobbles – those moments when you're tempted to go back and strike up a conversation with your ex – but stand firm and ask for help from those you can trust.

Do it for yourself and for your future. It'll be worth it.

One way to soften the blow of letting go of a past love is to accept that if the relationship is meant to work out, it will come back to you. Don't hanker after it or bargain with yourself. Don't tell yourself he'll definitely return if you take two months off. Release the relationship completely, or as best you can. Let go of any fixed outcomes and relinquish control. Hold on loosely to your dreams.

One technique I've used to help me let go of someone in the past is to write their name on a piece of paper and to put it in a special box I call my God box. This is where I put all the things I'm worried about or I can't find an answer to. You could have a Universe box, a Buddha box or a Mother Nature box, whatever works for you. You could bury your box in your garden and give that person to the earth or simply put the piece of paper with your ex's name on it in the soil. Let someone or something else work it out for you.

If the person does come back into your life, you'll be able to approach the relationship with a different mindset. In some cases, you'll wonder what on earth you saw in your ex and why you got so attached. In others, the attraction will still be there but you won't feel a desperate urge to rush in. You'll have a choice. You'll ask: 'Does this relationship meet my needs? Is it good for me? Is this what I want for my life?' rather than be consumed by an uncontrollable desire to jump into his arms.

Pause and reflect

- Do you deserve to break a mental tie with an ex?
  Be honest with yourself.
- Is the fantasy of what could have been taking up far too much headspace and stopping you from being open to somebody else?
- Are you ready to take steps to change this and how would you like to proceed?
- Would you like to put his name in a box or bury it?

Good intentions aren't always enough

I write all this knowing we are imperfect human beings rather than robots. I know only too well that years of personal development and all the self-awareness in the world can go out of the window when we're in the presence of someone we fancy like mad.

I know this because I've experienced it.

As I've mentioned, my partner and I had several break-ups over a period of five years until we finally committed to each other. We had a brief encounter when I was 40 and he was 45. This was followed two years later by a delightful three-month summer romance, after which we split up. We then had another short liaison the following summer that was closely followed by a break-up. Then, in October of that same year, we committed to each other, and we've never looked back.

After that first brief encounter, I didn't feel the need to go cold turkey. I wasn't obsessed with him and I was fairly sure he wasn't for me. But after our 'summer of love', as we called it, I decided I had no choice but to shut him out. I was clearly incapable of being near him without falling into his arms and I liked him so much I was thinking about him a lot. So I politely asked him not to call, text or email and I promised to leave him alone too. We managed it, aside from a few texts on New Year's Eve.

This silence and distance helped me free up some space in my head and heart so I could spend some time exploring who I was and what I wanted for my life. My partner told me later he'd found the silence hard, harsh even, and hearing that made me sad. But for me, there had been no other way.

Single again and with no lingering ties to anyone, I went

on a five-week solo trip over Christmas to Mexico, where I'd lived for five years in my twenties. I was determined to rediscover the spirited, courageous woman inside me who'd travelled the world alone. Initially, I was terrified – I no longer had excess food as my companion and it took me a while to find my feet. Eventually, though, I did.

The trip wasn't without romantic incident. I had a brief encounter on Christmas Eve with an Australian surfer dude after I broke my rule of no alcohol on dates and drank two beers. I also had a fling with a nomadic American. Neither left me feeling particularly good. But the rest of my holiday restored my faith in myself and in my ability to take risks.

Next came my solo camping trip to Spain where I steered clear of all romantic escapades, basked in the sunshine and enjoyed my own company. I was growing as a person, learning what healthy self-reliance looked like and pursuing my dreams without a man attached.

A few months after my Spanish trip, my partner and I spoke on the phone. I asked him what he wanted and he said he wanted to be with me and to live with me, and I realised I felt the same. We committed there and then.

So in my own relationship, I didn't quite follow the blueprint I've set out in this step. I stayed in touch with my partner during some of our break-ups and went back to him against my better judgement (at least at the time). There were a number of occasions when I berated myself for failing to keep my distance and for falling back into his tent at festivals as soon as it went dark. But I did gift myself some time away from him – time that allowed me to develop further as a person and to come to terms with what I really wanted out of life.

With the Tinder guy, the one I managed to get out of my house late that Saturday night, I did go cold turkey and it worked. There was a period, just after we'd split up, when I was totally obsessed with him but every time I wanted to phone him, I called a friend instead. She was walking a similar path to me – trying to act in her best interests in relationships as well. She reassured me that I deserved better and that better would come my way if I just held my nerve.

Months later, completely out of the blue, Tinder guy texted and suggested we meet up. My stomach did a somersault.

'Has he changed?' I wondered. 'Is he now ready for a more committed relationship?'

I dressed up and went along to meet him, feeling expectant. But no, he just wanted to say 'Hi'. Nothing had changed.

I waited for him to share his thoughts about our break-up – the realisations he'd had since we split – but our conversation remained at surface level. In fact, he seemed more interested in the dog at the next table and its attractive female owner than in me.

As I left the coffee shop, I felt relieved. I'd stood up for myself at the right time and I'd had a lucky escape. And he wasn't as hot as I remembered.

Breaking the cycle

If you're anything like me, short on willpower and a fan of instant gratification, cutting off contact can be a life-saving technique. But if you're prone to obsession and over-thinking, again like me, you may still struggle to get your ex or that fantasy man you never kissed out of your head.

Here are a few suggestions that may help break that cycle of repetitive, obsessive thinking about lost or imagined loves.

I've already mentioned the God box, which is a gentle technique you can use if you want to let go of someone for the time being but are unsure if you're doing the right thing.

If you know a bond must break, however, try writing his name on a sheet of paper, along with all your hopes and dreams for your future with him, then tear it into pieces and throw it off a bridge into a river or into the sea. Alternatively, you could burn the paper – fire is very cleansing, even if burning your ex's name feels like a harsh thing to do! You could write his name on the sand and let the waves wash it away as you allow the feelings of loss to wash over you, which is something we do on my seaside retreats, or find another ritual to signify the relationship is no more. You could also meditate and let the tears flow, knowing that connecting to your sadness is a key step on the journey to acceptance and letting go.

The thoughts may not disappear overnight but when they pop into your head, you can imagine the ritual you performed and remember the promise you made to yourself to detach from that person.

Our minds are like battlegrounds and if we can haul our thoughts away from what's obsessing us and onto healthier things, we'll stand a better chance of winning. This is why mindfulness meditation is so powerful. It trains our minds to focus on something such as our breath or how our body feels against the chair we're sitting on and to keep bringing our focus back to that every time our thoughts wander off.

Too often, though, we do the opposite – we allow our minds to focus on what's unhelpful. We indulge in thoughts of our ex, imagining how he looks or imagining his touch. We picture him sat opposite us in a restaurant or lying next to us and then we actively try to build the next scene and the next, until we're dressed in a white gown and walking down a church aisle.

Or is it just me who does this?

To borrow a phrase from my therapist, we make an entire movie out of a single scene rather than yelling 'Cut!' and shutting it down. So notice the next time you start making a movie out of a thought and do your utmost to think about something else. This takes discipline but discipline is something we can all develop.

I remember a time when I couldn't get an ex out of my head. I'd finished with him but I was still totally obsessed, doubting my decision, wondering if I should get back together with him. I didn't meditate back then but I knew I needed a way to break the cycle of repetitive thinking. So I decided to sing every time his name or face popped into my mind. I'd walk down the road or ride along on my scooter through London's streets singing, 'la, la, la, doo, doo, doo, la, la, la', sometimes at the top of my lungs.

I got some odd looks, but it helped.

Pause and reflect

- Can you relate to this pattern of obsessive thinking about a previous love?
- Would you like to try one of the rituals we've discussed to break a bond with an ex? Which one would suit you best?
- What other techniques might you use to get someone out of your head?

Figure out why you're holding on

It's also important to understand why you're holding on to a lost love and why you're struggling to find anyone else attractive, or even to believe there's someone out there for you. It may be because you like the comfort of his companionship or the sex, but it could also be a deliberate ploy on the part of your subconscious mind to keep you safe from real love so you can avoid potential hurt.

If our minds are stuck on someone who's not right for us, it can be difficult to think about or get involved with anyone else. That's convenient for those of us who are scared of loving and losing. But if you've done the work set out in the early chapters of this book, you'll be more aware of whether your subconscious is trying to keep you safe by blocking you from love.

No matter how hard it feels to say goodbye, no matter how much you want to kick and scream before letting go of an ex, a 'friend with benefits' or a fantasy in your head, please remember this truth: the more time you spend with the wrong person, the less time you'll have to spend with the right one.

I can't tell you the number of times I've wished my partner and I had spent the previous 10 or 20 years with each other. God willing, we have the best part of half a lifetime left to be together but what about all those youthful years when we were single or seeing someone else? I know this is fantasy because I know we wouldn't have got together back then – I wouldn't have been ready for this kind of relationship or we wouldn't have found each other attractive. But it's worth thinking about.

When you fall in love, you will wish you had more time

with that person, so clear the decks, break those bonds, let go of past relationships and free yourself up to meet your new partner.

In order to be open to meeting the right person, you will need to be aware of your dating trigger points – the things that push your buttons and make you want to run away – and you will need to know how to manage them. That's what we'll look at next.

Step Five: Reflection and action

- Reflect on whether you are holding on to a past relationship, physically or in your head.
- Ask yourself how this relationship is serving you.
- Begin to give yourself the love, companionship, comfort and security you were getting from that ex, or find someone safe to give that to you.
- Try putting his name in a God box or a Universe box, burying it in the earth or sending it floating down a river.

My reflections

Chapter 6

Understand your trigger points

'It is not worth the while to let our
imperfections disturb us always'
Henry David Thoreau

In the last five steps, you learned to look inside and feel your feelings, increase your self-esteem and identify and challenge any harmful relationship patterns or negative core beliefs. You also became willing to let go of lost loves, both physically and mentally, so that you are ready to meet new people.

You are halfway through your 10-step journey and you have done some great work on yourself (or at least you have set the intention to do the work after finishing this book).

At this mid-point, I think it's worth stopping for a moment to notice how you feel. Do you feel more grounded, more complete and more hopeful about your ability to find love and form a healthy relationship? Do you feel lighter, as though you have unpacked some of the baggage you were carrying or put down a heavy load? Do you notice an increase in your self-esteem and self-worth? Perhaps you are feeling healthier or even walking taller after spending time strengthening your core, both emotionally and physically. I hope you can see some positive shifts.

If you can't, don't worry. I imagine things have shifted but you might be the last one to notice. So believe that you are changing, and at the right pace.

Until now, you've been exploring your past, either on your own through stillness and meditation or with the help of others, such as counsellors, therapists, trusted friends, a support network or a community.

It is now time to move forwards and to put your healing and your emotional maturity to the test through dating. In other words, it's time to take this show on the road.

At this stage, it's important to be aware that while you're definitely on a new path, you may still be in for a bumpy ride – at least at first. When you choose a more spiritual way of being and start giving yourself the comfort, companionship and love you had longed to get from a partner, it can be easy to think that you are cured of all the beliefs and behaviours that used to block you from love. However, from my experience, the process of dating and forming relationships can push buttons we never knew we had.

This is why this step is about understanding our relationship trigger points so that we can survive the dating process and come out the other side with a healthy partnership.

Think of a trigger point as a circumstance or behaviour that stirs a strong reaction in us – one we may not understand or even notice.

As we get closer to the love and intimacy we long for, our fear often grows and our subconscious mind can find increasingly cunning and subtle ways to keep our hearts safe from potential hurt. As we begin to date, the voices in our head shout louder. They tell us we're not pretty enough or young enough or they tell us we've chosen the wrong person, or maybe we find other ways to sabotage ourselves.

So advance slowly on your dating journey. Avoid knee-jerk reactions or sudden decisions that may be based on fear.

Is it fear or instinct?

A question my friends and coaching clients often ask me is how can you know whether it's your instinct or your fear that's telling you to ditch a guy and run away from a relationship. It's one of the hardest questions I get asked and one I've never found easy to answer myself.

Is the churning feeling in your stomach telling you to finish it because this person isn't good for you or is your terror of commitment getting in your way?

The good news is that simply by asking the question you are on the right track. Having sufficient self-awareness and emotional maturity to look inside yourself and wonder if you are scared of intimacy will stand you in good stead. It's all too easy to assume it's our instinct that is telling us to bolt.

If you're not sure, it can help to talk it through with friends, a coach or a counsellor but ultimately, only you know the answer. You'll find that answer faster if you're well connected to your feelings and your intuition, as discussed in the earlier steps. Remember, though, that sometimes it's a case of trial and error. You're not going to get it right every time. Be prepared to sit with your decision until you feel more or less peaceful about it, then act on it and see what happens. You're more resilient now. Trust that you'll be okay.

If you're anything like me, peace won't come that easily to you. Ambivalence is one of my core traits – one I've had all my life. I've often felt as if I'm being pulled in two directions. I can trace that sensation back to my childhood when I felt torn between my mum and dad as their marriage broke up. Ever since I was small, I've also been scared to make a mistake. I am a perfectionist who has to get it right, so I have always struggled with decisions. If you're similar, don't give yourself a hard time. Make the best decision you can with the information available to you, knowing you can change your mind if you need to.

But the more you understand the things that push your buttons and prompt you to act in irrational ways, the more you'll be able to make healthy choices.

Understanding my dating triggers

For years, I had no idea that certain circumstances were triggering an extreme reaction in me and making me behave strangely towards partners. I thought my actions were entirely rational, despite the fact that my encounters with men often followed a bewildering pattern.

One minute, I'd absolutely adore a guy and I couldn't get enough of him. The next, I couldn't stand the sight of him. Suddenly, I'd see something in him that would repel me and the attraction would go out of the window. In that moment, I'd simply assume that I'd realised we were a bad match and it was time to move on.

I remember an incredibly tall Irish chap whom I'd initially fancied like mad. I loved his towering frame and sturdy, rugby-playing limbs. He took me on a romantic weekend to Donegal in Ireland where we met up with some of his friends in a country pub. Standing next to this gorgeous guy, I felt like the cat that got the cream.

A few weeks later, he visited me in London. It was a warm day and he was wearing shorts, showing off his muscly legs. Only I no longer saw muscles – I saw two chunky legs as white as milk bottles protruding from an unflattering pair of shorts. I couldn't bear to be with him after that. It was like somebody had flipped a switch inside me.

There was another guy I went weak at the knees for. We'd had a number of dates and everything was going swimmingly until he showed up on my doorstep one morning without having shaved and I spotted grey hairs speckled throughout his stubble (he was bald so I hadn't noticed any grey before). From that moment on, I no longer found him attractive and could only see his faults. Tiny things began to irritate me, from the way he crunched his cornflakes to the way he smiled, and I knew I had to end it before I said something mean.

I fell for another man on an outdoorsy weekend and we dated for several months but as I got closer to him, I began to judge him on everything from the way he walked to how much he ate to his relaxed work ethic. After a while, I had to call it off. I was convinced it had all been a mistake and that I needed someone more dynamic – and someone slimmer.

I cringe as I write those words, remembering how quickly I used to flip from being completely into a man to criticising him in my head or out loud. I now feel embarrassed by how judgemental I was towards boyfriends in my twenties and thirties. I also feel sad for those guys, even though I think they had a lucky escape – I wouldn't have made the best girlfriend back then. I imagine they didn't know what had hit them (if any of you are reading this, I apologise again). One minute, I couldn't get enough of them and then the next, I was back-pedalling very fast, dropping them like a stone or making some flimsy excuse about needing time out. I didn't understand what I was doing at the time. I had no idea I was behaving strangely. I simply assumed the guys weren't right for me.

Some of my behaviour reflects the push-pull pattern I identified in Chapter 3. I would reel men in, bring them close and then find a reason to push them away or my erratic behaviour and sharp tongue would force them to leave. This, as we've discussed, was a cunning defence mechanism on the part of my subconscious – a ploy to keep me safe from hurt.

However, I've come to understand there was something else going on in these relationships. They were pushing my inner buttons in a way I found excruciating. I was seeing something in these men that I absolutely hated in myself and I couldn't bear to see my most intolerable traits mirrored right back at me.

Excess weight is a good example. Throughout my late teens, twenties and some of my thirties, I wavered between being one to three stones heavier than I am now (that's 6-19 kilos for my metric friends) and I absolutely despised the layer of fat that enveloped my thighs, my upper arms and my waist and that dangled beneath my chin. I also hated the fact I was so weak and lacking in willpower that I couldn't resist the food.

When I was feeling fat, I'd hide my body under big baggy shirts and I'd steer clear of skirts or shorts. My weight was my nemesis. I couldn't bear to live with it but neither could I get rid of it, no matter how hard I tried. All the while, I was in denial about my binge eating. Even after I began recovering from my eating disorder and returned to my standard weight, I was still unhappy with how I looked. I would pinch and prod at my body, frown at myself in mirrors and berate myself because I no longer looked like the slim girl I was before I began to binge eat.

My eating disorder had left a painful physical legacy but it was also now wrecking my relationships. Whenever I dated a man with excess weight – chunky, white legs or a paunch – I saw myself reflected back. I saw my lack of willpower and my extra layer of fat. And I couldn't stand seeing either at such close quarters, especially not in someone I was trying to love. The experience sent shivers down my spine and left me feeling repulsed.

This never happened with my friends. I could accept my friends completely, no matter how they looked or how much willpower they lacked. But there was something about that intimate relationship with a man that meant I felt repelled when I saw myself in him. The same happened when I spotted the grey hairs in that guy's beard. I saw old age and I didn't want to date an old man or have to accept that I would be heading that way too.

If a guy acted needy towards me or if he was a people-pleaser who failed to stand up for himself, I also had a strong, negative reaction because I hated the needy, people-pleasing, weak and insecure side of myself.

Furthermore, I felt repulsed if I noticed something in a boyfriend that reminded me of the physical traits or personal qualities I'd disliked in my parents. This was because the small child inside me remembered aspects of her upbringing that had made her uncomfortable and when she came across them in a man, she felt vulnerable, scared or turned off.

Pause and reflect

- Can you relate to being in love one minute and feeling repulsed the next?
- Can you identify aspects of yourself you dislike?
- Have you spotted those qualities in the people you've dated and wanted to run a mile?

Understanding the mirror

I thought this pattern of fancying a guy and then feeling turned off by him would never change. It wasn't until I realised that I was reacting to unwelcome aspects of myself in him that I could take steps to manage my behaviour.

I came to understand that if I couldn't accept my weight, the way I looked or the age I was, I could never accept fat or signs of ageing in my man. And since everyone gets old, weight gain happens and perfection doesn't exist, I would be destined to be alone if I couldn't love my own humanness.

I had to integrate all parts of me rather than separate and split off the bits of myself that I disliked. I couldn't stay splintered – I had to see myself as a whole, flawed human being so I could accept a man's imperfections, even if they reminded me of the worst parts of myself.

As with other aspects of my journey, however, this was a gradual process. It took me a long time to learn to love the wobbliness of my upper arms or the excess skin beneath my chin. Even at 39, some seven years after I began recovering from my eating disorder, I was still finding things about my body to dislike.

I remember being at London's Southbank Centre a few weeks before my fortieth birthday at an event on eating disorders and body image. As I heard stories of girls and boys who were starving themselves, bingeing on food or self-harming in other ways, I felt enraged. This was my story too.

How much harm had I done to myself by wrecking my body and hating myself for so many years? Was I really going to carry on despising the way I looked into my forties and beyond? How many more times was I going to sit on the toilet staring disparagingly at my thighs, seeing if I could arrange my legs so they looked thinner or grabbing at my waist to see how many inches I could pinch? (That Special K advert has a lot to answer for.)

The event ended and my anger carried me home. Something had to change. I lay awake all night, thinking about the blog I knew I had to start writing as soon as it got light. The next morning, I launched my first blog, which I called *Just As I Am – An Experiment in Self-Acceptance*.

It was the first day of Lent and I declared on my blog that I would abstain from berating myself about the way I looked for 40 days straight and I would post about my progress every day. I would also stop beating myself up for my behaviours or any mistakes I thought I'd made. I would accept all aspects of myself and love myself fully, even if I failed to live up to my exacting standards.

Enough was enough. I was nearly 40, for goodness' sake.

I believe the process of writing my blog and abstaining from self-judgement consistently for that period helped me break the back of my destructive habits.

While I was learning to be kinder to myself, however, it would take me longer to extend this kindness to boyfriends and to accept and love everything about them.

Pause and reflect

- Can you identify any self-destructive habits that you would like to break?
- Do you judge your appearance harshly or criticise the quality of your work?
- Do you expect perfection of yourself and beat yourself up when you can't achieve it?
- Are you demanding of the men or women in your life?
- Would you like to change this? Would you like to go easier on yourself and on those around you?

Don't try to change them

When I first met my partner and in the subsequent years when we dated on and off, I found plenty of things to criticise about him. I disliked his laid-back attitude to life, seeing it as laziness and a lack of ambition – two qualities I hated to see in myself. I judged his long hair, his slight beer belly and his crooked teeth too, interpreting them as a lack of self-care, which was something I was guilty of and wanted to change about myself.

I also had a fragile ego despite all the inner work I was doing and thought his imperfect appearance would reflect badly on me. I remember reading that truly confident women are able to go out with men who are shorter than them or who aren't as good-looking as other guys because they are so sure of themselves.

There were also times when I saw aspects of my dad in my partner, some of which drew me to him while others pushed me away, depending on whether it was a side of my father I had loved or disliked.

In the early days, I wanted to change my partner. I wanted to improve him, instil in him a burning ambition or a drive to better himself. I wanted to turn him into something he was not. I especially wanted to convince him that he really did want to be a dad. And I wanted him to straighten his teeth, although I never said so out loud.

My partner didn't react well to my attempts to change him. He resented being some sort of improvement project. And why wouldn't he? I wonder how I would have felt if one of my boyfriends had tried to tell me I needed to be different, to work harder, lose weight or declare myself to be against motherhood. Writing that, it seems a crazy thing to do. But I did it and I imagine you might have done it too at some point, unwittingly or otherwise. Many of us were taught to keep striving and never to accept less than the best, from ourselves or from our boyfriends. Most of all, we understood we had to avoid *settling* for less than we deserved in a partner. In fact, we banned that dreaded word from our vocabulary.

Fortunately, I had enough wise people around me at the time to remind me that it was futile to try and change others and the only person I could change was myself. Every time I mentioned I wanted to fix or alter something about my partner, they suggested I ask myself what was it about me I disliked or wanted to change. They then advised me either to learn to accept and love that trait in myself or to do something about it.

So, if I wanted him to be more ambitious, I first had to accept that I lacked get-up-and-go at times and then I had to find more drive within myself for my own life. If I wanted him to do more exercise and lose weight, I had to love my body completely and then focus on my own wellbeing and the quality of my diet.

As I stopped trying to change my partner, he stopped feeling resentful and we grew closer. And as I held my critical and judgemental side in check, I became more empathetic and he became more willing to open up.

I remember one particular episode that really showed me how my critical nature had blocked me from true intimacy in the past and had come close to ruining this new relationship.

My partner and I were sat waiting for the chain ferry to cross back from the Isle of Purbeck to Poole on the Dorset coast and we were listening to Jeremy Vine's lunchtime show on Radio 2. The topic was teeth and Vine was speaking to people who had decided to wear braces as adults to straighten their wonky teeth.

Initially, the critic in me spotted an opportunity to hint to my partner that he might want to straighten his. But I knew not to start the conversation in that way, so I asked him if he had ever worn braces as a child. The school dentist had advised him to, he said, but he had refused because all the kids with braces got teased. Plus, his parents hadn't stepped in to explain why braces might be in his best interests in the long term. So his teeth battled for space in his mouth, some of them growing at different angles.

Hearing that story of the little boy who hadn't wanted to be teased turned my heart to mush. He had spoken his truth and shared his vulnerability and in that moment, I stopped judging his teeth. In fact, I fell in love with their uniqueness. Over time, I have also realised that my partner's teeth are strong and his gums are healthy while my gums are receding at an alarming rate, so I have shifted my focus to meeting my own dentistry needs rather than booking appointments for him.

I believe I was more able to show empathy to my partner because I had begun to show it to myself and he was more able to be vulnerable with me because I had softened and had stopped judging him. Empathy towards ourselves and towards others is a vital pillar of the falling in love process. We must learn to accept and love all of ourselves, even the bits we hate, so we can accept and love all of the person we end up with.

I am not suggesting there won't be days when we dislike aspects of our partner. That wouldn't be real life. But my problem was that my inner and outer critic never allowed me to get to the true love stage.

Using my upper arms as an example, I have spent years wanting to chop excess weight off them with a knife but I now accept my slightly larger arms as a unique aspect of myself. I also lift hand weights now and then to see if I can tone them up. Once we have embraced our looks, habits, anxieties and fears and made peace with ourselves, we can extend that empathy to the men or women in our lives.

So if you go on a date and the guy looks nervous or lacking in confidence, resist the urge to label him as a weakling you couldn't possibly be with. Instead, pause and look into his eyes. Why might he feel nervous? What childhood or adult experiences might he have had that knocked his confidence or damaged his self-esteem? Then, as you get to know him better, ask him about his life experiences with an open heart and bucket loads of empathy.

You will be able to do this if you have learned to empathise with yourself and to forgive yourself for any mistakes you believe you have made. You will be able to do this if you have fully accepted the way you look, feel and think.

In preparation for dating

We've established that empathy is key to healthy dating but empathy doesn't develop overnight, especially if you've spent several decades beating yourself up. In order to accept and love all of yourself and therefore to be able to accept and love a partner, you might need to put some effort in.

So take some time to notice and explore the aspects of yourself you most dislike. You can do this following a period of meditation or by writing in a journal.

Is it your fear, your weakness, your neediness, the size of your hips or the lines around your eyes that you hate? Is it your laziness, your indecision or your inability to resist cake or crisps? Is it your people-pleasing or your bad jokes?

Once you have identified the culprits, begin to love them. Speak kindly to yourself when you feel fear or when you struggle to decide which path to take. Forgive yourself when you overeat and soak your beautiful body in a bubble bath rather than punishing yourself. You could even try a period of abstinence from self-flagellation as I did over Lent. Incidentally, the biggest breakthrough in my recovery from an eating disorder was the moment I forgave myself for a binge and allowed myself to eat normally afterwards, rather than starving myself and sprinting around the park.

Love all of yourself with all your imperfections so that you can love all of your future partner, warts and all.

This is the new softness, the new mindset you want to take with you on dates. When you leave the house, suspend judgement and leave your inner critic at home. Tell yourself you are going to abstain from finding fault in the man you meet, just for that evening. Promise to greet him with an open heart and mind. By all means, look out for any warning signs and listen for alarm bells but refrain from picking holes in a perfectly decent guy.

Bear in mind that if you're tired, run down or feeling grumpy, it's going to be harder to suspend your critical side. When you're not at your best, you're likely to have less tolerance for yourself and therefore for those close to you. You may be especially picky if you're not feeling great so be aware of your energy levels when you go out on a date and be prepared to call it off if you're not in the right frame of mind. If you go ahead regardless, you may end up rubbishing someone who could turn out to be the person for you.

With plenty of empathy and your inner critic in check, you are now ready to move on to the next step: to let go of your classic type and throw away your 'must have' list.

Step Six: Reflection and action

- Does your attraction to a man or woman flip on and off like a switch?
- Reflect on the aspects of yourself you most dislike – this could a physical characteristic or a behaviour you berate yourself for.
- Have you ever seen your least favourite qualities mirrored back in someone you are dating? Has this turned you off?
- Can you commit to loving all of yourself? Can you commit to refraining from self-criticism and from judging people as inadequate for the first few dates?

My reflections

Chapter 7

Throw away the list

'*The more I know of the world, the more I am convinced that I shall never see a man whom I can really love. I require so much!*'
Jane Austen

At this point on your journey, I hope you've begun to understand why you find some people irresistible and why you find others a turn-off. I also hope you've started to explore why you might fancy a guy one minute and then discover you can't stand the sight of him the next.

These are valuable insights that will help you with the seventh step.

In this chapter, you are going to spend some time exploring your usual type. You are also going to begin to reassess the qualities you'd like to see in your future partner and become open to people whom you might have rejected in the past.

I wonder if you have a particular type that you go for and if so, I wonder how aware you are of that ideal and how it affects your choices. Do you favour men with a particular physique or personality? Is there a certain aspect of a man that you find irresistible almost every time? (I'm hoping that by this stage on your journey the 'unavailable type' no longer features in your romantic repertoire.)

The type you go for might not be as obvious as 'tall, dark and handsome' or 'red hair and green eyes'. It might be more nuanced than that. It might be more about personality or the way a man presents himself or behaves. Whatever you go for, the chances are that you have some sort of preferred type, so have a think about it for a moment so you can become aware of what it might be.

You might have a list of personal qualities that you would ideally like your man to possess. Those qualities could range from 'must have' to 'nice to have'. Even if you haven't written your list down, you might be carrying it around in your head or your heart and you might be making decisions about whom to date based on how many boxes on your list a man ticks.

It's likely that your attachment to a particular type and the length of your list of ideal qualities will vary depending on your age and stage in life. If you're a little older or have had a lot of relationships already, reality may have set in so you may have a shorter list and a more flexible idea of whom you would date. You may have realised that you can't have everything you want and that you're going to have to compromise on some things.

Alternatively, if you've had many failed relationships or long periods of singleness, you may have swung the other way. You may have begun to think you will never have anything you want or that you don't deserve to be with someone you find attractive. Hopefully, after all the work you've done in previous chapters, you will have begun to dismantle those negative beliefs.

My ideal man

As I write this, I'm remembering some of the items on the various 'ideal man' lists I've had over the years (these lists were both in my head and on paper, often scribbled in tiny notebooks with flowers on the front). My thoughts then turn to my partner, the man I absolutely adore, and I smile.

In my younger years, my type was anyone who reminded me of my dad or my brother. As I mentioned earlier, I was desperate to heal the hurts of my past and I wanted to feel close to the two men I idolised as a little girl. I kept seeking out their qualities in boyfriends and partners in a bid to replay my childhood movie and rewrite the final scene.

My dad and my brother loved me, I'm sure, but as a child, I felt I could never get as close to them as I wanted and needed. I longed for them to love me with abandon, but the love that came my way never felt enough. Perhaps that was because my need was too great – the hole I was asking them to fill couldn't be filled by anyone or anything on the outside – or perhaps they struggled to connect with their own emotions and therefore with me on a deep level. Whatever the reason, it felt like I was always chasing after them, my arms outstretched, grasping for something that was just out of reach.

When my dad moved out of the family home and married again a few years later, I felt as if he'd slipped even further away from me. He only lived around the corner, drove me to school and came to cross-country training with me most Saturdays but the facts didn't matter. My mind told me I'd lost him and so I set out to do all I could to win him back – by achieving as much as possible at school and by looking as thin and pretty as I could.

Next, my brother moved out. He was a year older than me so he went off to college at 18, leaving me in Liverpool with my mum. On the day he moved to Derby, I gave him the record 'He Ain't Heavy, He's My Brother' by The Hollies and we played it over and over in his room while I sobbed. Poor guy. Soon, my brother had a girlfriend and more interesting things to do in his holidays than come home so I felt as if I'd lost him too.

These early experiences with the main men in my life explain why it felt strangely familiar and comforting to me when a guy was emotionally distant or just out of reach. I could recreate my childhood feelings by dating men who were unavailable in some way.

I was also drawn to guys who reminded me of my dad or brother in other ways. They were both more than six feet tall, good-looking, musical, sporty and funny, so they set the standard high. I'd often go for musicians because my dad played the guitar and banjo in Liverpool's Merseysippi Jazz Band (The Beatles supported my dad's band in the Cavern Club before the Fab Four hit the big time, a claim to fame I would share when I wanted to impress). My brother played in a band and sang too.

So if I spotted a man carrying a guitar case, I'd go weak at the knees and if I saw him strum and sing, I'd swoon. Humour and showmanship attracted me too because my dad and brother were entertainers who made people laugh and they loved being on stage.

Sportiness was another quality I went for, partly because both the men in my life were good at sport but also because I was too. I'd always been an outdoor type who loved fresh air and exercise.

This attraction to men who are familiar to us is inevitable. Each of us will be drawn to partners who remind us of the significant people we grew up around, in looks or in values (or in some cases, we'll be attracted to people who are the exact opposite). It's also inevitable that we will seek out people who we think can meet some of our unmet childhood needs.

I took this to extremes, however. When I met someone who reminded me of the men from my early life, I spotted a golden opportunity to restore the losses I'd experienced in my past. I wanted to get close to my dad again, so close that we would merge into one. I wanted to make him love me above all else. I wanted to make him stay.

Pause and reflect

- I wonder if you have been searching for a replacement father figure or seeking to heal your childhood wounds through your adult relationships. I wonder if you have been trying to replay the movie of your past so that you could create a happier ending the next time around.
- I wonder if your usual type reminds you of your dad or another significant male from your youth. Or is he the opposite?
- Take a moment to think about your type. It's good to become aware of why you are drawn to certain traits or to a particular type. By gaining more awareness, you may feel you have more of a choice about the people you're attracted to. You may also become open to people who don't fit your ideal type.

It was love at first sight

As I mentioned, my dad and brother set the standard high when it came to their physique, their humour, their creativity and their various other talents but I also put them on a pedestal. As a child, they seemed perfect to me and I couldn't see any faults in them. That's why the men I met had so much to live up to – and why they generally fell short.

When I was 16, another man walked into my life, or rather he shimmied his way in, and it was love at first sight. His name was Johnny Castle – the entirely masculine but incredibly tender dance instructor from the 1980s hit movie *Dirty Dancing*.

Johnny, played by Patrick Swayze, was almost too much for my inner romantic to bear.

I loved his solid, unshakeable frame, his firm grip and the way he swept Baby (Jennifer Grey) off her feet and lifted her above his head in a pristine lake. I loved how he slowly undressed her in his cabin, revealing her perfectly tanned, toned tummy and ultra-white underwear (I wanted to look like Baby as well as kiss her on-screen man). And I loved the fact he came back for her so they could have one final, show-stopping dance, because while Johnny had huge muscles, he also had a big heart.

I was hooked. I needed to know how it felt to be lifted out of the water in a see-through white blouse or to be guided around the dance floor with Johnny's hand in the small of my back. I wanted to know what it was like to lie in his bed, his arm around me and my head on his chest. I too wanted to hear the record player's needle click onto vinyl and say to him breathlessly that I was terrified of leaving his cabin and never feeling the way I felt when I was with him again.

So as Johnny and Baby kissed on the dance floor and the credits rolled, I made a silent promise to myself that I would find my Patrick Swayze, fall in love and feel what Baby felt.

There were five school girls in the cinema in downtown Liverpool that night but I believe I was more susceptible than my friends to the fantasy of the perfect man. This was due to a combination of my innate sensitivity, a deep insecurity and the hole my dad had left when he moved out.

I so needed to be lifted aloft. I so wanted to be saved.

So that's how Johnny Castle got added to my 'ideal man' list and mixed in with the character and physical attributes of my brother and dad. No wonder nobody could tick all my boxes after that. I had built a fantasy in my head about the perfect bloke and I couldn't imagine being with anyone less than him. This was yet another ploy on the part of my subconscious mind to protect me from getting close to a real man in the real world and risking my delicate heart.

To give you an idea of my 'ideal man' tick-list, here's a summary of what I was looking for:

- Good-looking (naturally).
- Taller than me (definitely).
- Sporty, with a thirst for adventure and a love of the great outdoors.
- So funny he could make me cry with laughter.
- Intelligent (obviously).
- Emotionally intelligent – in other words, in touch with his feminine side without sacrificing any of his Hugh Jackman-like manliness.
- Gentle and caring.
- Committed, faithful and reliable.

- Different – he needed to have some sort of 'edge', perhaps a colourful past like me.
- Unconventional in some way.
- Skilled at DIY and always willing to have a go.
- Good at languages (if possible), especially Spanish as I am fluent.
- Good at dancing, preferably salsa and swing but Ceroc would do, as long as he could lead me round a dance floor with a strong grip and hurl me over his shoulder when required.
- Available (of course).
- Willing to become a wonderful father to the children we were going to have together.
- Young and fit – he could win bonus points by being either younger than me or, if not, fit and energetic enough to look after our future kids, because I was getting a bit old to run around after them.

Was this really too much to ask?

Letting go of ideals

After many years of trying to find this impossible mix of a manly, masculine, straight man who could swing his hips to salsa tunes like a slim, diminutive Latino and speak Spanish to me as he put up the shelves, I gave up. He may well exist but if he does, he's probably married to his Spanish dance partner.

These weren't the only traits on my list that had to go. I had other preconceptions that were past their sell-by date too. I had studied at Oxford University and travelled the world with Tony Blair so I thought I deserved to be with an Oxbridge graduate who'd had an equally high-flying career. I imagined my partner would be 'A' type like me. He would be ambitious and driven – perhaps a medic, an army officer or another journalist who earned a good salary and had a nice flat in Marylebone or better still, near Hampstead Heath.

I also thought my man would be outgoing and gregarious, someone who loved to party and liked to be the centre of attention. It seemed, in hindsight, I was looking for a carbon copy of myself.

But that was before I went through the process of transformation outlined in this book. That was before I dropped the mask and became the person I am rather than the person I thought everyone wanted me to be.

As I recovered from my eating disorder, got in touch with my feelings, learned to meditate and left my high-stress Reuters job, I softened and slowed down. I spent more time cooking at home and less time running around town. I took more baths and less showers and bought candles and spiritual books.

My priorities changed too. I no longer wanted to spend my life at work and I was over climbing the career ladder. I wanted more time to relax, to have fun and to be outdoors.

Inevitably, the list of qualities I wanted in a man also began to change.

Now that I had more time on my hands, why would I want to be with an ambitious lawyer or a medic who worked around the clock and would never be home? Why would I want to go out with an adrenaline junkie now that I was calming down?

As I matured emotionally and nurtured my inner oak, filling the hole inside me with self-love and faith, I threw away my lists and began to focus more on values like kindness, gentleness, loyalty and trust.

Is he enough?

I was 40 when I first met my partner. I was on the journey towards emotional maturity by then but I wasn't that far along and I still had some fixed ideas about whom I should be with. That's why my first reaction to him, after the initial attraction had died down, was that he was not *enough*. He had studied at Portsmouth Polytechnic and his only experience of living abroad had been a year spent in Hong Kong, which I decided didn't count because he'd gone with a girlfriend, not on his own. He worked as a design engineer in a clock-in, clock-out job and didn't seem to aspire to anything more. He seemed quite content with his lot.

Yes, I had changed and calmed down but I hadn't lost my ambition – I was always striving to better myself, to achieve more and to do more interesting work. I never felt satisfied with my life so I couldn't possibly be with someone so laid-back.

I remember when I first went to his office. I saw a tatty-looking windowless box in a car park (it doesn't look as bad as that) and in that moment, I decided I couldn't possibly go out with someone who worked there. What would my friends and peers think? Surely I was better suited to a man who worked in a shiny, glass skyscraper in Canary Wharf, just along from the Reuters headquarters?

As it turned out, my partner is exactly what I needed and we couldn't be better matched. I didn't need someone with the same level of drive as me or whose emotions were wired in the same way as mine. I am a person of extremes. One day, I'm deliriously happy and filled with joy, dancing around the kitchen to Radio 2. The next, I'm stuck in a murky hole and it can take me a few days to climb out.

My moods range between high and low – there isn't much middle ground. I feel things intensely, good or bad. I love deeply but I get easily hurt.

My partner, on the other hand, hums along somewhere in the middle. There are no major emotional peaks or troughs, very few tantrums and rarely any tears. He is emotionally steady and physically sturdy, very much like an oak. He is the perfect counter balance to my personality and I am to his. He is the Yang to my Yin.

I lift him up a little so he's hovering just above the middle while he grounds me, calms me down and brings me back to earth. Sometimes, when I can't sleep, I place my hand on his back and try to absorb some of his peace and stillness. Or if I'm agitated, I throw my arms around his broad shoulders and hold on tight.

What a gift.

He reminds me of who I am at my core and of the things I truly enjoy. I imagine I will always be someone who strives for more but I also love to take time off, exercise outdoors and sit on the beach. My partner's job isn't glamorous or high-flying but it's suited to his personality and it pays him enough to go snowboarding and windsurfing, and to buy a kayak and a good tent. He finishes at five o'clock every night so he can spend time playing with his outdoor toys and doing the things he loves.

He is also far more intelligent than I ever knew – perhaps more than me or in a different way. He is a walking encyclopedia and is often amazed by the gaps in my knowledge, despite the fact I studied at Oxford. When it comes to languages, though, he's way out of his comfort zone. We joke around with Spanish and French phrases at home but he's not a natural linguist. Years ago, I gave a boyfriend a hard time because he didn't pick up Portuguese as quickly as me. Thankfully, I've changed. I no longer judge.

I don't judge my partner's poor spelling either, although I did at the start. This might sound silly but if I hadn't gone on my own journey of self-acceptance and developed empathy, I would never have been able to stay with someone whose spelling wasn't great. I am a writer, after all. But these things don't matter to me in the slightest anymore. They're part of his uniqueness and I love him for them.

Nor does it matter that my partner dislikes dancing, hates Latin music and thinks salsa steps are a bit like falling over. I can go dancing on my own or with friends.

Best of all, my partner has his own strengths, a few of which were on my original 'ideal' list: he's fantastic at DIY, very handy with a drill and he loves to have a go. He's practically minded and does his own car mechanics, dressed in oily overalls. He also shares some of the qualities I saw in my dad and my brother: he likes exercise, loves being outdoors and he makes me laugh. He can be a little emotionally distant and he finds it difficult to connect with or talk about his feelings, but my compassion and vulnerability make it easier for him and he has no problem saying 'I love you'.

Most importantly, though, my partner is there. He is always there.

He is there at the station when I get off the train from London or Winchester. He is there when I come home late from a work event. He is there when I need to have a cry, even if my tears make him feel uncomfortable. He is there on the weekends when I want to have fun with him. He's there at my side when I go swimming in the sea or he's standing on the beach holding a towel for me if it's too cold for him to go in.

He is there.

And deep down, when I think about it, that's all I ever wanted. I wanted someone who would be there, with me and for me. I wanted someone who would stay.

What I have discovered is that as we grow, develop, age, recover and become more self-aware and in tune with our hearts, we start to realise that the qualities we thought were important – the qualities we thought our man absolutely had to possess – aren't that vital at all.

In fact, if you're anything like me, you'll probably learn that there are other traits that are far more suited to you. As you become more centred and whole, you'll begin to see that what you thought you wanted from your man isn't what you actually need from him. Your priorities will change.

If you talk to married couples or long-term partners, you'll often find their other half is the last person they expected to be with or is someone they dismissed for years until they were mature enough to see their true worth. That's definitely the case for me.

So I wonder if it's time for you to reassess your list or to throw it out.

Pause and reflect

- Do you have a written or mental list of the qualities you would like to see in a partner? Are those qualities the same as yours or do they complement your strengths? Most importantly, are they in line with your values?
- What values are important to you – kindness,

generosity, faithfulness, freedom or family values? What really matters to you? Is it his job or his status, how he looks, how much he earns or where he lives? Or is it his gentleness, his good heart or his reliability? Ask yourself what you truly need.

- When answering these questions, begin to form a vision of the person you would like to be with. I prefer the idea of a vision to a list these days because I believe in setting intentions and creating a vision for my life.

- To set your intentions, write down, draw or imagine a broad-brush vision of your future. Where do you and your partner live? What activities do you enjoy doing together and apart? What values do you build your shared life around?

No more Mr Right

By now, I'm hoping you've let go of the idea of Mr Perfect or Mr Right and have come to understand that this fantasy of an ideal man could be a cunning ruse by your subconscious to keep you out of relationships entirely so you stay safe from hurt.

If the people you meet are never good enough, clever enough, handsome enough or successful enough, that means you don't even have to try and date them. You don't have to risk your heart. The part of you that desperately wants to protect you from pain will pull the wool over your eyes and convince you that you haven't met the right man yet.

Try to see that search for perfection for what it is – a barrier to intimacy and a survival tool that has served its purpose but that now must go. You are ready to take a chance. You have strengthened your inner oak, become more resilient and more discerning. You are in a much better place.

If you're resisting this step, if you're thinking that you deserve the absolute best and you're waiting for your soulmate, I understand that. But the man who is the absolute best for you may not look like your ideal partner. He may have a different physique, complexion, profession or outlook to what you imagined.

So be open.

While we're on the subject, a quick word about the term *soulmate*. The Guardian got its marketing right when it called its online dating site Guardian Soulmates. That name will certainly appeal to those who believe in 'The One'. My partner is absolutely the man for me but I don't sign up to the notion of 'The One' and I think this idea of *soulmate* can be misleading.

I believe that meeting someone who is right for us is all about timing. It's about where we are in our lives, how far we have come on our emotional journey and how ready we are to commit. Yes, attraction is vital too but timing plays a part in that.

My partner and I could have met years ago. In fact, I think we might have been travelling in Australia around the same time when we were both in our twenties. But I don't think we would have been attracted to each other back then, even if we had met and both been single. I probably would have found him too steady and dull and he might have found me too crazy and self-destructive. We needed to meet at the right time and in the right place – a time and place where we were willing to push through the Ordeal phase so we could get to the Real Deal.

I could say my beautiful Spanish boyfriend was my

soulmate for a number of years, even if our relationship was unhealthy in some ways. When we were in our twenties and living in Mexico, we were totally aligned in terms of our crazy, fun, spontaneous and sometimes self-destructive behaviours. But it would never have worked out – after we split up, he began to date men and came out as gay.

For me, the word *soulmate* conjures up something that's almost too good to be true, a meeting of minds and bodies – a merging of two souls. This hasn't been my experience of real-life relationship. It's much messier than that.

I'm not suggesting you accept less than you deserve but I am suggesting you be mindful of the deceptive myth of the perfect soulmate or the fantasy of Mr Right. Yes, feel the sparks and the romance at the start but know that for many of us, love is a choice that we make with our faculties intact and our feet planted firmly on the ground. It's a choice that involves commitment and compromise.

Pause and reflect

- Do you believe in the idea of 'The One' or of a soulmate?
- How do you feel about the idea that love is about timing and about where we are on our emotional journey when we meet someone?
- Looking around at the couples you know, which theory rings the most true?

Are you too good for your own good?

Even if you have grown out of the fantasy of Mr Right, it could be that your high standards are keeping you single. Women who have created great lives for themselves often suffer from what I call 'the curse of the capable woman'.

We have beautiful homes, fantastic careers, great holidays and healthy bodies. We are financially independent and socially active. We go travelling at the drop of a hat. We've learned to do our own DIY or if not, we have a long list of reliable tradespeople at our fingertips. And if we've done the work in the earlier chapters of this book, our lives are now fuller than ever and we feel good about ourselves. We don't really need a man anymore.

While this is a great place for us to be in terms of healthy self-esteem, it's worth noting that this fierce independence and extreme competence can both put men off and block us from opening up to them. We are protective of who we let in, and rightly so. We're not prepared to share our wonderful lives with anyone or to *settle* for somebody who isn't our match. But be aware of how you interpret this idea of *settling* – it can be a red herring. As high-achieving women, the word makes our skin crawl but our resistance to it can cloud our judgement and make us blind to potential partners who are more gentle, more straightforward, more reliable and less 'A' type – people who are actually good for us.

So relax your independence a touch. Try to be less strident and less fearsome. Many men like to be depended on. They like to feel useful. They like to wear the trousers. I'm not suggesting we tie ourselves to the kitchen sink, just that we soften a little bit.

Why not challenge yourself to send a message online to someone you wouldn't normally choose? Or why not go out on a date with someone who is different to your usual type – someone who doesn't tick *all* of your boxes?

Then, give him a few dates, three or four or even six. Let

the relationship grow. Let some warmth come into your heart. Don't judge him. Give him the benefit of the doubt.

If you feel you haven't got time to soften, slow down and give someone more than one chance to impress you, the eighth step on this journey will help. In the next chapter, we are going to look at how to get our priorities straight and how to make time for love.

Chapter Seven: Reflection and action

- Have a think about your usual type. Does he or she remind you of significant people in your childhood?
- Do you have a list of 'ideal' qualities, either in your head or written down, and how realistic is this list?
- Try creating a broad-brush vision of the person you would like to be with – draw it, write it down or imagine it.
- Spend some time in meditation and then ask yourself what qualities you would really like to see in a partner.

My reflections

Chapter 8

Make time for love

'Dost thou love life? Then do not squander time,
for that's the stuff life is made of'
Benjamin Franklin

In the first half of this book, you did some transformational inner work so that you could enter into dating and relationships with solid foundations. Then, in the last two steps, you began to look outwards. You explored the things that push your buttons and cause you to have knee-jerk reactions to certain people and you threw away your list of 'must have' qualities so you could see beyond your usual type.

I wonder if you've had the chance to put what you've learned to the test on a date.

Let me guess, you haven't had time.

You've been too busy at work. You've been running around trying to do a brilliant job or trying to keep everyone around you happy. In fact, you've barely had time to meet your basic needs, to eat and to sleep, never mind to explore love.

I can relate to that.

We looked at busyness at the start of this book. We discussed how we fill our lives with constant activity or around-the-clock work, always striving to do our best. For many of us, this busyness serves a purpose – it means we can avoid feeling any pain or hurt that might surface if we take a moment to sit still, and we can sidestep the challenges of dating and relationships. By staying busy, we don't have to risk our heart, face possible disappointment or expose our self-esteem to potential knocks.

Work was my favourite way of staying busy. As a person of extremes, I don't do things by halves. So for many years, I gave my all to my work and I gave nothing, or almost nothing, to my personal life. By my late thirties, I had an impressive CV and a job title to die for but no partner and no family.

How on earth had I ended up here?

I wonder if that rings any bells for you.

For ambitious, high-achieving women and men, work often takes precedence. We work through weekends and into the night. We miss social engagements and show up late to parties. Perhaps, if we studied a career like medicine or law, it took us years even to qualify. We hoped we'd meet someone on the job, because that's where we spent most of our time, but for many of us, this didn't happen.

So here we are, accomplished and financially independent with a responsible profession and a reasonable salary, trying to figure out where the last two decades went and how we managed to miss some key life stages. Or we're separated, divorced or widowed with children, wondering how we're going to find space in our frantic schedules to do our inner work, never mind to go on dates.

That's why this step is about learning to manage our time. It's about getting our priorities right and making time for love.

What's driving your ambition?

When I look back through my teens, twenties and much of my thirties, my main life goal was to achieve as much as I could. My ambition and my drive kicked in very young. In previous chapters, I mentioned some of the core beliefs that I formed in my childhood. Notably, I believed that academic and career success were the way to my father's heart and that love wasn't something my clever head should worry about. I remember my step-mum telling me after Dad had died that he'd have loved me even if I'd ended up sweeping the streets. That brought tears to my eyes. I hadn't known that as a child. I'd picked up a different message.

Compulsive work and the accolades that followed also helped to fill the hole inside me, in the same way as the food, while the status that came with being an international journalist bolstered my low self-esteem (and terrified me at the same time).

When I arrived in Mexico in my mid-twenties, I began climbing the career ladder. I worked on a couple of English-language newspapers and then got a traineeship at the American news agency Bloomberg. I worked my socks off and became a correspondent. My next goal was to work for Reuters and to move to Brazil. At the time, I had been dating my Spanish boyfriend for a few years but I barely gave our relationship a second thought when I applied to Reuters in São Paulo. I got the job and my boyfriend decided to follow me there, but I would have gone without him. Maybe I knew our relationship wasn't right but nevertheless, I was single-minded. My career came first.

A few years later, I set my sights on a bigger prize. I wanted to return to Britain and I longed to return in style. I wanted to come home after 10 years living abroad to a triumphant fanfare and to be able to say, 'Look Dad, I've arrived!' I landed the sought-after role of UK political correspondent for Reuters and took up my desk in the reporters' gallery of the Houses of Parliament. I had done my parents proud.

However, I wasn't satisfied. I still aspired to become the next Kate Adie, the BBC correspondent I had seen on TV in China's Tiananmen Square in my final year of school. I wanted to be on national television – then I could say I had really made it. I applied to the BBC, ITV and Sky News and did television work whenever possible for Reuters. I made some TV appearances, reviewing newspapers and discussing politics, but I didn't manage to land a reporting role with a broadcaster. I was still trying in my mid-thirties.

So my work consumed me for several decades. I was a perfectionist and I spent hours trying to get my stories just right, then worried through the night about what I had written. I also felt like a fraud so I had to work doubly hard to prove myself and to disguise the fact I wasn't supposed to be in that job at all. Despite my Oxford education and global career, I was the daughter of a single-mum from Liverpool and I never felt I belonged in the corridors of power.

It wasn't until I broke down and got signed off work at 36 that I began to realise how much I had prioritised my career over other areas of my life.

My transformation was gradual. Even after I took voluntary redundancy and became self-employed at the age of 37, I still felt I had to prove myself. I took on new projects without pausing to ask myself what I really wanted to do next following many years as a news journalist. I even went back to a different branch of Reuters and worked four-days a week, reporting on disasters and emergencies. That role took me to Haiti to cover the devastating earthquake of 2010. I was still an adrenaline junkie and my work still came first.

I was also driven by a deep-rooted sense of financial insecurity, which had always been there no matter the size of my pay packet or the value of my London flat. I feared I would end up on the streets if I didn't work hard.

I was a tough taskmaster, a workaholic and a busy bee. I had some short relationships in my thirties but it took me a long time to grow and develop emotionally and to carve out some space for love.

In fairness to myself, I'm an intelligent, creative woman so naturally I wanted to put my gifts to good use but there was something else going on – due to my emotional baggage and my fear of getting hurt, I didn't *want* to make time for love.

All my striving took me to great heights but in the end, I felt empty. I remember waking up single and childless on my 41st birthday and looking around my Islington attic flat with its wooden floors, natural fibre carpets and colourful mementos from all over the world.

'What have I been striving for? What was all that about?' I asked, as my tears dripped onto my Calvin Klein pyjamas.

There was nobody there and the silence was deafening.

When work always comes first

There's another scene from a few years back that highlights my skewed relationship with work.

I was 42 and I had booked an appointment at a Harley Street IVF clinic to have my fertility tested. They were going to measure my anti-mullerian hormone levels (also known as

AMH), which indicate how many eggs you might have left. After that, they were going to count the number of follicles on my ovaries.

I'd booked my fertility MOT (as the clinic called it) for a number of reasons. I wanted to find out if there was still a chance of me conceiving a child or if the motherhood ship had sailed. My results would help me know whether it was worth trying to meet a man who wanted kids or not.

I also wanted to see if the process of testing my fertility would stir any desire to have a child with a sperm donor and to be a single mum. This course of action had never appealed to me, probably because my mother brought me up on her own, but I was running out of time to meet a guy.

Finally, I was taking the test for professional reasons. I was writing a book that explored my feelings around motherhood after turning 40 (I still hope to finish and publish that book) and I was researching an article on fertility testing for *Easy Living*, a women's glossy magazine.

The appointment had been in my diary for a while but as the date approached, my work piled up. I was struggling with deadlines and I decided I had to postpone the test.

I dashed off an email to the clinic to move my appointment. That email still makes me smile but it saddens me at the same time. It's classic me – at my most rushed, putting my work before my personal life as I'd done so many times before. I sound like I'm juggling too many balls.

Here's what I wrote:

My work has piled up – I have a deadline this week – and I think it's going to be really difficult for me to get to the clinic for an AMH test this week. You had me booked in for 3 pm tomorrow and I was also going to try and come sooner, which I haven't managed. It's going to be too stressful for me to get there tomorrow, which also means I'd like to postpone my April 16th appointment/scan etc. as I won't have my AMH results ready in time. Is that possible without any penalty? If so, could you cancel both appointments for me and I can ring in a week or so and reschedule when my work is less hectic.

Can you hear the sense of overwhelm in my writing?

So I'm 42, childless, with a desire to have a family and I'm postponing my fertility test for a number of weeks to meet a work deadline. I can now see the irony in that. When I finally got to the clinic the following month, I arrived late after sprinting down Harley Street and I hadn't filled in the medical forms they'd sent me in the post. I'd had no time.

I wonder what I could have done instead, given I had a genuine deadline. Perhaps I could have asked for a few more days to finish the piece of writing I was due to hand in, although the idea of asking for an extension hurt my pride. Or perhaps I could have decided that my 80 percent effort was good enough and I didn't have to strive for perfection. Maybe I could have planned my schedule better in the first place, so I had a healthier work-life balance.

But no, I cancelled my fertility check-up and got back to work.

Of course, I may have been scared too and therefore reluctant to take the test (my results were average for my age, by the way, so not great). But if I had been less busy with my work and had learned to manage my time in a more loving way, I might have been able to process those fears, have a cry, maybe ask for help and then face them.

Pause and reflect

- Can you relate to waking up alone on a significant birthday and asking yourself where on earth you went wrong?
- Can you identify what is driving your professional ambition? Do you have low self-esteem or suffer from imposter syndrome? Are you hiding from uncomfortable feelings or a sense of loneliness?
- Have you skipped social engagements, arrived late at parties, missed friends' weddings or cancelled dates because of work commitments? Are you always in a rush?

Are you investing in dating?

When it came to dating, I didn't invest much time. I didn't have time to give a guy the benefit of the doubt or to go on a second or third date unless there was a real spark. I rarely had the time to even meet a man face-to-face. I felt too busy to look through profiles on the dating sites I was paying my hard-earned money to be on. If the site didn't have an app that I could check on my phone when I was on the bus or the train, I'd barely look at it at all.

I spent little time creating my online profiles. I recall a dating coach I interviewed asking me how much time I put into writing CVs for jobs I wanted compared with the time I dedicated to crafting a profile to try to find love. She had a point.

But I spent most of my day sat in front of a computer because I worked so hard. Why would I want to spend my evenings and weekends doing the same? It didn't occur to me to reduce my work hours to carve out space for dating and relationships.

Truth be told, I had little inclination to invest time in my romantic life. Aside from all the fears and blockages we've discussed, I resented having to work at it. Surely love should just fall into place?

After all, I'd ticked all the other life boxes and in the right order (or just about). I'd done as I was told. I'd been a good girl. I had worked hard at school, won a place at university, got my degree, got a good job, become financially independent and bought my own flat. Yes, I had gone off the rails for a while but I had put down my unhealthy crutches and was back on track now.

Love was the natural next step.

I looked for it everywhere, in supermarket queues, in the adjacent seat to mine on airplanes and at friends' weddings but it never showed up – not until I shifted my priorities, learned to make myself happy and created space in my life to do the things that made my heart sing.

Get your priorities right

I was in my early forties when I decided to dedicate more time to my personal life both by dating and by doing activities that brought me joy and expanded my social circles in an organic way. I was still working hard, but all the personal development I'd done was helping me take my foot off the gas.

I signed up to the dating app Tinder and I actually managed to meet up with a few men rather than just chat online. One of those dates went well and turned into the short relationship I wrote about in Chapter 4.

I also joined a London hiking group that organised day trips and weekends away. I had got back in touch with my love of being outdoors and the hiking group offered me the chance to meet new people while being out in the fresh air.

Walking in the countryside would also give me a taste for what it would feel like to live out of London, even if I was only doing day or weekend trips. I still hadn't found the courage – or the time – to follow my heart to the coast but I had the seaside in my sights.

On my first day hike, I had a good chat with a single guy whose profile I'd seen on Guardian Soulmates. There were no sparks but I returned feeling hopeful – I had enjoyed a day out, met some fun people and, as a bonus, I had come into contact with a single bloke. I was on the right track. Coming home, I took the big step (at least it was for me at the time) of signing up for a weekend trip to the Isle of Wight with the same group.

In my younger years, I did that kind of thing all the time without thinking twice about it but I was over 40 now. I had got used to my own space, to peace and quiet and to sleeping in a comfortable bed. On the trip, we would be travelling down in shared cars and sleeping in dorms of eight. I have never been a great sleeper. I have a hyperactive mind that likes to mull things over through the night and I'm very sensitive to noise so I had huge reservations. I also assumed everyone else on the trip would be in their twenties. But I decided to ignore the voices in my head, get over myself and just do it. Even if I barely slept for two nights, I could catch up on sleep when I got home.

I needn't have worried. On that trip, I met a fun bunch of people who were around my age, laughed a lot and hiked in the sunshine along a stunning coastline. I slept like a baby in the dorms and came home feeling refreshed. I also met an attractive man who was interested in me. Result! I felt younger, braver, more positive and less set in my ways when I got back to London.

That flirtation didn't come to anything but that's not the point. I had been courageous. I had tried something new. I had challenged my preconceptions about sharing lifts with strangers and sleeping in dorms. I had stepped out of my comfort zone. I had identified a need to spend more time in the outdoors and to meet new people and I had met that need, despite my fears.

I wonder if you feel set in your ways or stuck in a routine. I wonder if you would like to challenge some of your preconceptions and broaden your social circles while doing the things you love.

Whether or not you return from your hiking weekend, your painting workshop, your Ceroc class or your choir practice with someone's phone number isn't the key here. Going out and doing something you love will do wonders for your self-esteem.

In fact, I believe the act of doing these new activities will slowly change the way you feel about yourself, thereby improving your relationship prospects. So try to make time for them.

One thing leads to another

I met my partner after a spell of prioritising the things that made my heart sing.

One April, one of my university friends invited me to a small music festival in Wiltshire after someone dropped out of the trip. We would go on our bikes and we would camp. It sounded right up my street and I said 'Yes' in a flash, but soon the voices in my head tried to talk me out of it.

'You've got too much work to do,' the voices said. 'You'll have to cycle through the crazy London traffic with a tent and a sleeping bag on the back of your bike. You'll be cold at night and you won't be able to sleep. You'll be too tired to do your work on Monday. You'll overeat on your tiredness and then you'll hate yourself and get depressed.'

Within minutes, my mind had turned a weekend in Wiltshire into a disaster movie.

It's true, it was a bit of a pain cycling through London with stuffed panniers and a tent tied on top. I was right about the cold too – I was freezing in my sleeping bag, so cold that I got up every few hours to refill my hot water bottle in the toilets. But none of that mattered. I laughed more than I had in years.

We met a group of guys on the campsite, drank beer and wine (or they did – I think I abstained) and spent the night trying to make coffee on a camping stove by torch light, giggling every time someone knocked the coffee pot over, spilling its entire contents onto the grass (that happened a few times). The next day, we went mountain biking and ate scones with jam and cream.

I was exhausted when I got home but I also felt excited and happy.

One of the guys we met on the campsite went on to become a good friend. In fact, he's now married to my university pal who invited me to the festival.

Another bonus was that I connected with a group of like-minded, sporty ladies who, a few months later, invited me on a cycling trip to Padstow in Cornwall. I met my partner that May bank holiday weekend. He was one of their friends.

I had followed my heart, made space for the things that brought me joy and challenged the negative voices in my head that told me to stay home. I hadn't expected to find love but five years after that Cornish trip, my partner and I bought a house together in Poole.

I believe in a natural order of things. I believe that if we spend time laying the foundations for a healthy partnership and then prioritise our joy, we will feel happier, healthier and more attractive. We will feel younger, lighter, more courageous and more resilient. We will be more willing to go on dates and to speak to guys in coffee shops or on the bus. We don't have to study dating apps for hours or go on four dates a week. Some of us may not even need to date at all. It might all fall into place when we do what we love.

Pause and reflect

- Are you spending time doing the things you love or are you stuck in an unhealthy routine? Maybe you want to paint, draw, sing, travel or hike. Make time for that.
- Observe how you feel when you do what you love. Do you feel more confident, more open to dating or more willing to talk to people when you're out?
- Notice the voices in your head that try to talk you out of following your heart and challenge them. What's the worst that could happen?

Ring-fence the good stuff

I wonder if you're feeling some resistance right now. I wonder if you're thinking you simply don't have time to do the activities you love or to date. Perhaps you have a full-time job, kids to look after on your own or an elderly parent who needs your care.

I acknowledge your frustration but please hear me out.

We all have the same amount of time. Nobody has more than 24 hours in a day or 365 days in a year. I accept some people have more commitments than others, especially parents of young children, but in many cases, I think it's less about time and more about courage.

At least that's how it was for me.

In Step Two, we explored the topic of self-esteem. We looked at how some of us have a habit of saying 'Yes' to others and saying 'No' to ourselves. We feel that tap on the shoulder that's telling us to leave work on time to get to a party, a Pilates class or a date, but our boss puts a project on our desk or an urgent email arrives and the promise we made to take care of ourselves or to make space for fun goes out of the window. We put our handbag down and get back to work.

I did this for years. I didn't know how to put myself first. I didn't know how to keep my time boundaries, with myself or with others. I was too scared to speak my truth.

I heard an anecdote a while ago about a high-flying banker who used to swim twice a week. He ring-fenced his swimming hours and protected them fiercely. Whenever someone tried to schedule a meeting with him during his time at the pool, he declined, no matter how important it was. He said 'No' to others to say 'Yes' to himself. Swimming was vital to his mental and physical health. He had his priorities straight and he respected his own time boundaries.

In contrast, I've had very weak boundaries and I've felt pulled in all directions. I've been foggy about my priorities and unable to say 'No' to others so that I could say 'Yes' to myself. That's one of the reasons I have struggled to finish a book.

I've been writing my other book for four years but I never felt I had the time to focus on it. I always had other work to do and money to earn. I would write bits of it now and then, but I kept getting sidetracked. I also lacked the courage needed to finish a book. I hadn't matured enough emotionally to face my perfectionism and push through my blocks.

Then, in January 2017, something changed. I decided I'd had enough of abandoning my creative dreams and of ignoring my desire to write. I was tired of seeing other people publish books when I had been writing professionally for 20 years. I was a few months off my birthday and I decided I wanted to have a book in print before I turned 46.

I made it my absolute priority and, as I did, I found time I never knew I had.

I took out my diary and began to cross things off. I cancelled appointments, postponed workshops, moved things around, sent out emails with apologies and said 'No' to catch-ups and coffee dates. For a people-pleaser like me who doesn't like letting people down, this required courage but my goal was worth it.

I became protective of my days and ruthless with my time. I went for this book like I've rarely gone for anything before.

It was a liberating experience.

There's an irony here, of course. I've just been telling you to work less and make space for your personal life but as I finished this book, I did the opposite. I confess that my self-care went out of the window. My car almost ran out of petrol, I got right down to the rim of my only lipstick and I didn't get to the beach for a few days. Worst of all, my poor partner barely saw me. I felt like I was back at Reuters, getting up before dawn to finish a story and working well after dark.

There were some important differences, however. This time, I was working hard at *my* dream rather than working for a boss or making money for someone else. This was something I had wanted to do for years. I also knew it was for a short period of a few weeks so my frantic pace was just about sustainable. Nor was I bingeing on food as I wrote. In fact, I was so engrossed in my writing I sometimes forgot to eat. And finally, I had a partner now. Yes, I neglected him for a while as I finished the book but we're talking days not months or years. I didn't wreck my relationship – although it did become alarmingly clear to me how little time I must have had for my personal life when I worked crazy hours as a news journalist.

If, like me, you're a perfectionist and a person of extremes who's passionate about your work, be aware of how your dedication to your career might be affecting other aspects of your life, especially the area of love.

You may discover that old habits die hard, as I have found out with this book, but awareness is the first step to change.

Pause and reflect

- Can you relate to saying 'Yes' to others and saying 'No' to yourself, especially where your career is concerned?
- Are there any costs involved in subordinating your needs and putting other people first? What is the price of being nice to others while being unkind to yourself?
- What activity or goal would you like to ring-fence?
- What could you take out of your schedule to make space for your dreams?

What do you really, really want?

My priorities are different now to when I was in my twenties and thirties. That's the same for many of us. Love is at the top of my list – it didn't really feature before.

At the end of my life, I want be able to say that I loved deeply and wholeheartedly and that I held nothing back. I want to say that I took a risk with my heart, that I exposed myself to loss but that I reaped incredible rewards.

I also want to have made a difference somehow. I want to put my talents to good use. I want to create something and leave a legacy. But most of all, I want to love.

I imagine you know what loss feels like. You may have lost a parent, a sibling, a partner or a friend. It hurts, doesn't it? It hurts because you loved them so much. But would you have loved them any less? Love is what it's all about. As the French novelist George Sand said: 'There is only one happiness in life, to love and be loved'.

One way to identify what you really want out of life is to think about what you would like the inscription on your headstone to read or what you would like people to say at your funeral. I don't mean to be morbid but looking forwards to the end of your life will help to sharpen your focus and give you courage to create the kind of life you want to live today.

Spending time in meditation will also help you connect to the desires of your heart. Try practising mindfulness for 30 minutes or an hour – you deserve to give yourself plenty of time to understand what truly matters to you.

After your meditation, do some free-flow writing about the things that are most important to you. Write down the activities you most enjoy, the ones that make your heart sing. Remember the things you loved to do as a child. You could also draw what comes to you. As I've said, I love to fill a page of A3 with colourful pictures and words. My drawing usually has images of camper vans, the seaside and sunshine and words like *freedom*, *love*, *travel* and *adventure*. These are the things that make my heart sing, so this is how I want to spend a lot of my time. You could try creating a vision board as we discussed earlier in the book.

It's also a good idea to do a time inventory to find out how you are spending your hours. Over the course of a few weeks, jot down how much time you're spending at work, doing your life admin, dating, commuting, surfing the internet or doing acts of self-care. This is your opportunity to get clear about where your time goes so be honest with yourself. If you discover you spent two hours on Facebook one evening, write it down and then ask yourself if that's a good use of your time. Before I start working with coaching clients, I ask them to do a similar exercise. Often, they admit to spending zero hours on romance, only a few on wellbeing but over forty on work. We then try to redress the balance.

Once you have your time inventory in front of you, use it to map out your diary for the following week. Allocate time to the things that are important to you and leave out unfulfilling tasks that suck away your time. Perhaps you'd like to add in activities that will expand your social circles such as a dance class or a hiking trip.

After reading this book, your inner guide may be prompting you to see a therapist or a coach, join a support group or try out a spiritual or faith community. Listen to that voice and make time for that in your schedule. It could help you on your journey to love.

If you're feeling creative, you could mark segments of the day or week in colour in your diary to represent different activities. For example, you could mark the weekend in yellow for leisure to remind you not to do any work and you could add chunks of green for anything to do with wellbeing You could also shade some hours in red to represent dating (or another colour if you prefer, but maybe not black – we're feeling hopeful now!).

Remember, you're going to need courage in order to respect your time boundaries. So pause and reflect whenever somebody gives you work or asks you to do something that's going to be a drain on your time. Then flex your inner oak and answer honestly and courageously.

If you are still doing the groundwork outlined at the start of this book, set time aside in your diary for that.

Then, when you are ready to date, do so with commitment and purpose (not with half-heartedness but not with panic or desperation either). Give this side of your life the importance it deserves. If you're dating online, spend time creating your profile and messaging potential dates and then make space to meet them. If you can't bear to do internet dating, cancel any subscriptions you have and invest your time and money in activities that will bring you joy and expand your social circles.

Also, make sure you take time to draw up some loving guidelines for yourself so you can go on dates *and* protect your precious heart. We'll be looking at how to do that next.

Step Eight: Reflection and action

- Have you missed opportunities to go on dates or meet new people in the past because you have prioritised your work? Are you ready to change that?
- How are you spending your time? Is 80 percent of your time spent at work or on similar commitments or do you have a good balance between your personal and professional life? How would you like to shift the balance?
- Choose an activity, write it down in your diary and then ring-fence it. Protect that chunk of time ruthlessly. Notice when you break your commitment to yourself and celebrate when you don't.
- Decide how many hours in a week you would you like to dedicate to going on dates or to doing social activities that offer the opportunity to meet new people. Maybe start small and build up.

My reflections

Chapter 9
Set boundaries for dating

'Daring to set boundaries is about having the courage
to love ourselves even when we risk disappointing others'
Brené Brown

By this stage on your journey, you're hopefully feeling more confident, more sure of yourself and more complete as a person. You're spending less time at work and more time doing the things you love, or at least you have set that intention. You've identified your priorities and made space for your dreams. You like your own company more than before and you've become someone you would gladly date.

You haven't got everything sorted. You have your emotional wobbles and difficult days – days when you forget to take care of yourself, when you put others first and when you pay the price for being too nice. You haven't quite reached inner oak status yet. But you feel stronger inside than you did at the start of this book and you are moving in the right direction, knowing it's about progress, not perfection.

That's wonderful, but then you go on a date with someone you find irresistible or you get physically entwined with a lovely man and everything you've learned goes out of the window as your hormones kick in and the mist descends.

Your imagination begins to wander, hurtling off like a runaway train, leap-frogging a number of relationship stages until you can picture the two of you shacked up in a cottage by the sea or doing the tango in Argentina as part of a world tour. Either that or you imagine a sparkly ring on your finger or a large bump in your tummy. As Jane Austen wrote in *Pride and Prejudice*: 'A lady's imagination is very rapid; it jumps from admiration to love, from love to matrimony, in a moment.'

In this trance-like state, your powers of discernment dwindle, your willpower disappears and your inner oak turns to cardboard. On this fluffy cloud, you are no longer a competent individual with a full life and a vision board full of hopes and dreams.

Instead, you're like a tiny sailing boat, tossed around on a choppy sea. You've lost your anchor. Or maybe you're a woman overboard.

I lost my anchor many times in the past. I forgot who I was at my core and I let my imagination run away with me. This was especially true in my late thirties and early forties when my biological clock was ticking like crazy and I was running out of time to have a child.

It sounds so clichéd, so anti-feminist, so unfitting of an intelligent, educated, successful woman, but I could quite easily come away from a first or second date picturing my wedding or imagining what kind of baby our mixed genes would make.

You see, I'm a hopeless romantic at heart, brought up on a steady diet of movies like *Dirty Dancing*, *Notting Hill* and *Four Weddings and a Funeral*. More importantly, I bear the deep childhood scars we talked about earlier that make me vulnerable to fantasy.

Eventually, after many mistakes and mishaps on dates, I realised I needed to find a way to rein in my over-active imagination and to stop my brain from turning to mush if I was going to stand any chance of choosing a partner wisely. I also had to find a way to control my hormones and keep my clothes on for as long as possible to stop the dreaded mist from short-circuiting my intelligence.

I needed to learn to date with healthy and loving boundaries. This is our ninth step.

Delaying gratification

I was in my thirties before I came across the term *boundaries* in relation to dating, friendships and relationships. I knew about boundaries on cricket or football pitches but I wasn't aware that I could have emotional and physical boundaries with myself and other people – in other words, limits to help me act in my best interets and protect myself from hurt.

Good parents understand how to set emotional and physical boundaries, even if they don't use the term. They know when to say to their children: 'No, you've had enough chocolate now' or, 'You can watch an hour of TV provided you do your homework first.'

Children, from toddlers to teenagers, push against these boundaries. They want their own way. They want to test the limits and see how much they can get away with. Often, they don't understand why they can't just do as they please because they don't yet know how to differentiate between what's in their best interests and what's harmful to them. If they're reckless teens, they may be aware that something is going to hurt but they'll want to do it anyway. Parents who have time, emotional intelligence and maturity will be able to explain to their offspring why these boundaries are important and gradually their children will learn. As they mature into adults, they will be able to discipline themselves.

Some parents struggle to set boundaries because their parents didn't know how to set limits with them or because they are overwhelmed, exhausted or depressed. They allow their children to do as they please, sometimes because it's easier or it seems kinder that way. This means their children never learn the gift of moderation or how to delay gratification. These kids then move into adulthood with their inner toddler or teenager still running the show.

This was my story. I didn't learn how to set boundaries with myself and I didn't learn to restrain my instincts. I discovered early on that excess food could take the pain away and that alcohol, compulsive work and male attention could make me feel better too. But because the hole I was trying to fill was a bottomless pit, no amount of food, alcohol, success or affirmation was ever enough. I never felt full up. The hole needed to be filled from the inside or through spirituality – it was love-shaped or God-shaped. Instead, I was trying to fill the void with substances and external validation.

My hunger for love was so great that the concept of self-discipline bypassed me. I became addicted to the high I got from the sugar or the other stuff. I lost the ability to have just two biscuits, one slice of cake or two gin and tonics. Luckily, I had a strong survival instinct that kicked in just in time so I never pushed myself over the edge. Either that or someone was looking out for me.

When I began to recover from my eating disorder and other compulsive behaviours, I had to learn about boundaries, self-discipline and delayed gratification from scratch. I had to learn to parent myself so I could allow myself a treat every now and then without devouring an entire slab of chocolate, a whole box of muesli or a large pot of organic yoghurt (I binged on healthy things too).

With alcohol, I had to moderate my intake or cut it out entirely because booze would inevitably lead to a food binge. At work, I had to learn to accept that the story I had written was good enough and send it off to the editor as close to my deadline as possible and to switch the computer off when my eyes began to go square (I struggled to do that when finishing this book).

Then, as I dated, I had to learn to set loving guidelines and healthy boundaries for myself. I had to learn to exercise some form of self-discipline and to restrain my instincts wherever possible.

I was terrible at this, absolutely dreadful, so I understand if it's difficult for you too. But we can but try and awareness, as always, is the key.

Staying more or less sober

Ever since I was a teenager, I had dated drunk. This was both accepted in Britain and it was almost expected. In fact, you were considered odd if you didn't drink to excess when out on a date.

For many of us, alcohol helps break the ice but I often drank more than I could handle and ended up in situations I regretted. By my mid-thirties, though, I was drinking a lot less or nothing at all, determined not to trigger a food binge.

My friends got used to me being teetotal – I like to think I was just as much fun when I was sober – but dating without alcohol was a challenge.

If I met men online, they would often suggest a drink. Usually, I resisted the temptation to explain my life story in an email. Instead, I would suggest a coffee date (I no longer drank caffeine either but I could have a peppermint tea) or I would go along and have a lime and soda. Sometimes, I'd be mature, authentic and brave and say I didn't drink, or not very much. On other occasions, especially if I fancied him and thought my non-drinking would put him off, I'd make up some excuse about an early start the next day or I'd make sure I'd gone out on my Vespa so I couldn't drink. The more I worked on my self-esteem and the more I told the truth, however, the easier it got.

Anyway, if we needed alcohol to get on well then what hope was there for the future? And if my non-drinking put him off then he wasn't the guy for me, right?

That sounds like I've got it all sorted, doesn't it? But it didn't always go smoothly. I'm human after all and I have even less willpower than some of my fellow human beings. Plus, I'd only just learned about boundaries so I couldn't be expected to stick to them every time.

My very first snog with my partner was after a small glass of red wine. I had told myself I wouldn't drink and I'd vowed I wouldn't kiss him. Two boundaries broken in one night, which wasn't surprising because alcohol generally got me into trouble.

I also broke my 'no alcohol on dates' rule when I was on the solo trip to Mexico I mentioned earlier in this book. I sat down in a restaurant in Puerto Escondido with an Aussie surfer dude I'd met that same afternoon and ordered a Corona beer on an empty stomach, despite having decided in the taxi on the way there that I definitely wasn't going to drink. I ordered a second beer before the food came and before I knew it, I was back at his place. How on earth did I get myself into that mess again? I was over 40. Hadn't I learned my lesson by now?

Head. Brick wall. You know the score.

Pause and reflect

- Take a quick look back over your dating history. Are there times when booze has got you into bother?
- Would you benefit from limiting your alcohol intake on dates or from not drinking at all in the presence of someone you're getting to know?
- Remember, this is a great opportunity to put your emotional maturity, your self-esteem and your inner oak tree to the test. And if alcohol is a deal breaker for him, is he really someone you want to be with?

Keeping it brief

Another boundary I set for myself was around how long I stayed out on a date. If possible, I tried to go on coffee dates or for a walk along London's Southbank, both of which allowed me to avoid the alcohol problem. They also helped me to limit the date to a few hours and to get home before dark. That way, there was less temptation to take things further than I wanted to on a first encounter.

I had learned that I found it easy to fall for a man before I even got to know him so I put boundaries in place to take care of myself. I may have wanted to kiss him but I knew it would be wise to delay gratification, to go away and think about it and to start afresh another day.

Sometimes, I'd arrange to meet a guy at six o'clock and then a friend of mine at eight, meaning I had no choice but to end the date at the agreed time.

Short dates with time boundaries also meant I didn't have the opportunity to spill my entire life story on the first meeting because over-sharing was another habit of mine. I thought if he knew more about me or about my struggles he would like me more or we would feel closer to each other. It was a way of reeling a man in, winning his affection and creating a false sense of intimacy. Short dates stopped me from doing that.

I also made a decision to keep my backstory to myself in the early days of a courtship. I committed to myself and to my friends that I would keep the conversation light on the first few dates with a guy and steer clear of topics like depression, addiction or angst.

I tried to avoid the subject of babies right at the start too, although it wasn't always that easy. If you definitely want to have children, you deserve to find out as soon as possible if the man is on the same page. It may not be clear from his online profile so you may need to ask the question. It's your call as to whether you want to mention this on your first few encounters or wait until later. I found it was often a case of trial and error.

Rules, of course, are there to be broken and I crossed my boundaries on many occasions. Once, I was enjoying a guy's company so much that I lost track of time and missed a phone call from the friend I was supposed to be meeting later. When I eventually called her back, she heard how much fun I was having and agreed to stay home (she was tired so it suited her too). So my coffee date turned into dinner and a later night than planned. Fortunately, there was no alcohol involved so I got the bus home at eleven o'clock. No harm done, although I was besotted with him by the end of that long date. Our courtship ended a few weeks later.

Meeting face-to-face

As soon as I understood that I was prone to romantic delusions and to fantasy, I also tried to limit the number of times I emailed or texted a man before I had met him face-to-face. These days, it's so easy to play ping-pong text late into the night or to send emails for weeks before you even meet. But I had learned the hard way that sending messages back and forth often built a false sense of intimacy, fed my vivid imagination and sent my inner romantic skipping off through the daisies.

When I was in my twenties, I emailed a mystery man for weeks. He knew who I was and got in touch with me first but I didn't know him. He wrote beautifully, though, and after a while, I was convinced this was the man of my dreams. I created an image of him in my head – how he would look and the sparks we would both feel. But when we met, my heart sank and my fantasy came crashing down. He wasn't how I'd imagined him to be. What's worse is that he really liked me. He was bitterly disappointed and bewildered when I switched from sounding besotted with him over email to being cold and distant in real life. As I shut the relationship down, I felt like the worst woman in the world.

The push-pull dynamic we discussed earlier in this book

was clearly going on here. I reeled him in and hooked myself in too, then as soon as we were close, I withdrew. But our email exchanges had also created an illusion of intimacy and the notion of a relationship that didn't actually exist. We were living in a fantasy world – me even more than him because I didn't know who he was.

I learned from that experience and from others to limit the number of texts or emails I sent before I met someone face-to-face.

Pause and reflect

- What time boundaries would you like to put in place around dates? Would you like to keep your first dates to daylight hours, make plans to meet a friend afterwards or set a time limit, albeit a flexible one?
- Can you relate to my experience of building a fantasy image of a man in your head before meeting him? Would you benefit from setting some boundaries around virtual communication? Would you like to limit the number of messages you send in the early stages of a relationship?
- It's trickier with long-distance relationships but if you're dating someone who lives far away, first ask yourself whether you're attracted to the fact he's unavailable, at least geographically, and second, commit to speaking on the phone once a week rather than texting constantly.

Rein in your thoughts

If, like me, you have an over-active imagination and a tendency to romanticise situations, it's also a good idea to set boundaries around your thinking. Earlier, I mentioned my tendency to take a thought and make a movie out of it. I could create a whole series of scenes and a beautiful ending from one simple encounter.

For example, after a positive experience on a first date, I would write a script in my head that would feature our first holiday together. I would then imagine our honeymoon in the Seychelles as the credits rolled. If this sounds familiar, it's a good idea to exercise some self-discipline with your thinking. As soon as the movie starts to roll, cut the scene, send the actors home and think about something real instead.

My thinking could go in two directions, however. I would either dress him in armour and mount him on a white steed or I would rip him to shreds in my head before we'd even ordered our drinks. I would come up with a whole list of reasons why the man sat in front of me wasn't good enough, smart enough, tall enough or funny enough. I would make up excuses along the lines of: 'I could never go out with anyone who lives in Basingstoke'; 'I couldn't date a builder'; or, 'I couldn't possibly end up with someone who wears slip-on shoes'. (My partner wore slip-on shoes on our first date. They may even have featured in my list of reasons for breaking up with him the first time around. He still has them and I like them now. In fact, I wear them to hang the laundry up outside.)

Okay, so we all have our standards, our likes and our dislikes, but when critical thoughts come into your head, stop for a moment and ask yourself whether you're searching for reasons not to like him. When you judge someone instantly, you can't see beyond that thought and it puts a barrier between the two of you. That means you're no longer listening when the builder says he wants to construct his own home in the countryside or develop a property empire. And it means you've switched off by the time the Basingstoke guy tells you he wants to move to the seaside and buy a bolthole in your favourite part of London.

So why not set some firm boundaries around your thinking? As you leave home, vow to suspend judgement for the entirety of the date, and then the next date and the next, until you see through the surface stuff and begin to warm to him. You never know, you might just fall in love. You might not but you can guarantee you won't fall for him if you criticise him from the outset.

I wonder if you're able to give men a break and allow them a bit more time to make an impression on you. Of course, you need to be connected to your intuition and you need to listen out for alarm bells. You know what your patterns are by now so if you have a habit of dating abusive or unavailable men, you need to look out for red flags and leave as soon as you can. But if your date is falling a bit short of your expectations, if he's less confident or less chatty than you would like, give him a break. Go on a few dates. Don't rule him out.

Remember what we said about empathy and compassion a few chapters back? Guys can lack confidence or feel nervous too, especially in the presence of successful women, but that's not a reason not to give them a chance. We're all human. We all have our issues. So don't say goodbye before you've given him an opportunity to come out of his shell or to stop spouting nonsense. He might be feeling anxious.

My partner and I have wonderful conversations these days and we really make each other laugh, but I remember sitting next to him at dinner on our early dates and thinking he didn't have much to say. He wasn't loud enough or Alpha male enough, or so I thought at the time.

As it turns out, he's exactly the man I need in my life. So give your date a bit more time, enough for you both to feel more comfortable and more confident with each other and for some connection to grow.

If you're a man reading this, I can imagine it might be hard to date women who seem to have it all together on the outside. But remember, many of us are vulnerable inside. Sometimes the confidence is just a mask. And we would like to see your vulnerabilities too. We find them endearing.

It is also worth noting here that we are all imperfect beings with our own idiosyncrasies and that the men in our lives have to come to terms with *our* uniqueness and deal with *our* crazy ways. I used to be so focused on what I didn't like about a guy that I'd forget there might be things about me that could put him off.

My self-esteem swung between two extremes. Sometimes I'd think I was the least attractive woman on the planet while other times I'd think I was the most eligible thirty-something in town. In my mind, I was the one doing the choosing, not him. What's not to like about me?

But men have choices too. Maybe they don't love my gregariousness or the amount of angst I carry around. But are they prepared to roll with it? Are they willing to give me the benefit of the doubt and to arrange another meet-up? I have a feeling men are more open to doing this than women

– or at least than I was in my dating days. And I'm certainly grateful that my partner decided to accept me as I am rather than judge me on my failings.

Reining in our inner critic is even more important when we get closer to a man and move into the Ordeal phase of the relationship, as we discussed in Chapter 3. If we're scared of commitment and intimacy, or if we're terrified of loving and losing again, our subconscious mind will invent all sorts of reasons why this relationship needs to end. We'll pick holes in him in our head and out loud. We'll tell him why we think he's not good enough or why he needs to change. Most men balk at this and I can understand why. Being told you're not good enough or feeling like you're some sort of improvement project would get anyone's back up.

I remember an ex saying to me once that he didn't think anyone could ever meet my standards or be good enough. I feel sad about that. Although my relationship with my partner has proved him wrong.

In my experience, criticising a man out loud or trying to change him into something he's not is a sure-fire way to create distance in a relationship and to push it to breaking point. And that's exactly what my subconscious wanted to achieve to keep me safe.

I have had to learn to keep my mouth firmly shut. I have had to learn to bring the focus back to me every time I want to criticise him. What aspect of myself is he mirroring back to me and why do I hate that side of me so much? Can I learn to accept and love that characteristic in myself? We looked at this in Chapter 6. If I want him to work harder, it's probably because I am not achieving what I want to achieve. If I want him to earn more money, it's likely because I feel financially insecure. And if I want him to lose weight, it'll be because I'd like to shed a few pounds. I deserve to put my own house in order rather than throw stones at his.

So begin to see your tendency to criticise and judge for what it is – a ruse to keep you out of relationships and to stop you from having to look at the things you dislike about yourself.

Keep your options open and your clothes on

If you have a tendency to fall in love hook, line and sinker on a first or second date, it's helpful not to put all your eggs in one basket.

I used to aspire to date as the Americans do. I had girlfriends in the US who would go on three or four coffee dates with different men and carry on dating a range of guys a number of times before they settled on one. I'm not sure they used the phrase *going steady* like they do in the movies or sitcoms but it seemed they went on multiple dates and then made a choice to commit to one guy and to see where the relationship went.

This seemed a much more sensible approach than mine, which was to go on one date, kiss a guy, marry him in my head and then struggle to think about anyone else.

The crux of the problem was generally the kiss and whatever came next.

My downfall was my lack of physical boundaries on dates. Once snogging or sex entered the equation, my aspiration to date like the Americans died a death. The blinkers went on and I could no longer see anyone other than the man right in front of me. Nor did it feel morally right to keep my dating options open once I had got physical with a guy.

Physical intimacy changed everything. My ability to discern what was right for me or make decisions in my best interests disappeared. My willpower dissolved. I could no longer hear my intuition or, if I could, I could no longer muster the courage to follow it.

Eventually, of course, I did find a way to reconnect to myself and to extract myself from a man's arms, but it was generally too late. I'd given too much of my heart away. I'd got hurt or I'd hurt someone else. I'd wasted energy and time.

I kept making the same mistakes and getting the same results until I got tired and learned my lesson. Some of us have to learn by doing.

If, like me, you have weak physical boundaries and tend to end up entwined after promising yourself you weren't going to touch a guy, it's a good idea to find a dating buddy or an accountability partner − a friend to check in with when you're out on a date. Connect with someone who's on the same journey as you, someone who's also trying to set loving boundaries and keep them, and share the promise you've made to yourself. At the end of the evening, let them know how you got on. This is also good for safety. Or if you feel yourself getting into trouble during a date − perhaps you've had too much wine and you're hovering around your danger zone − nip into the toilet and phone your friend.

Remember, sex changes the relationship in a big way. The hormones and chemicals that get fired up when we have sex or get physical with someone are powerful ones. So try your best to restrain your instincts until you are sure and get yourself some support if you don't think you can hold your boundaries on your own.

Pause and reflect

- Have a think about any physical boundaries you would like to set before you go out on dates?
- What kind of support network would you like to put in place so you can keep your promises to yourself? Is there a friend you could ask to be your dating buddy?

Boundaries in the early stages of relationships

You've been on a number of dates and you've decided to give a relationship a shot. You have moved into a different phase of the dating process. At this point, it's tempting to spend every second with each other. In many ways, this is quite natural, but it can also throw your healthy routine into disarray.

By now, you'll have got used to having some quiet time every morning to connect to yourself and to meditate. You may have taken up a new hobby and hopefully you've increased your self-care.

Your inner oak is expanding nicely but then this relationship comes along and messes everything up. Your mornings are no longer your own, you don't have time to meditate and you start cancelling some of your favourite activities so you can spend time with him.

As I say, this is inevitable at the start. You are in the bonding phase. It's a magical stage and a time to be enjoyed.

But it's important to put some boundaries around your time and make sure you keep up your self-care routine as best you can, otherwise you can lose yourself in the relationship and forget who you are. This makes you vulnerable. The connection with your boyfriend takes on too much importance. You start to lose touch with some of your friends and stop doing some of the things that bring you joy and boost your self-esteem.

You can become more sensitive in the relationship too. You can become clingy, more attached to it working out and worried about what would happen if it broke down. Your life can go from being quite full to being focused on this one partnership and that can be unhealthy. You may also become less attractive to your partner as you lose sight of the things that were nurturing your inner oak.

By all means, throw yourself into the relationship if it feels right but maintain your sense of self and hold on to some of your routine. Make sure you spend at least one evening a week alone at home, soaking in the bath or reading a book and getting up early to meditate or to connect with yourself in another way. Meet up with your friends, go back to your choir or get to that salsa class you enjoyed. Don't merge your life with his. Keep some of it separate. Maintain some of your independence.

Then, as you grow closer to him while holding on to your sense of self and keeping up with your self-care, start to discern whether this person is really worth investing in. And if the answer is 'Yes', make a bold choice. That's our final step.

Step Nine: Reflection and action

- Boundaries come in many forms. Ask yourself which boundaries are the most important and urgent for you. Think about boundaries around time, alcohol, your thinking or physical boundaries.
- Write them down and share them with a friend or a dating buddy.
- Notice every time you break one of your promises to yourself. What was going on for you in that moment? Did your hormones kick in or did you feel the need to please someone else? Were you afraid of disappointing the person you were with?
- When you uphold one of your boundaries, celebrate in some way. Take note of it, treat yourself somehow or buy yourself a gift.

My reflections

Chapter 10
Make bold choices

*'Twenty years from now you will be more
disappointed by the things that you didn't do
than by the ones you did do'*
Mark Twain

You have arrived at the final step on your journey and you are about to reap the rewards of all the hard work you've done so let's take a moment to look back and see how far you've come.

You have connected to your feelings and learned to tune in to your intuition or to a power greater than yourself; you have increased your self-confidence and sense of self-worth; you have identified and removed some of your emotional blocks and challenged your unhealthy patterns; you have let go of lost loves, become aware of your relationship triggers and replaced your 'ideal man' list with a more realistic vision; you have created space in your life for love and for the things that make your heart sing; and you have set loving guidelines to keep you safe on dates.

You are now ready to make some bold choices.

Before we delve into this step, let me tell you a little bit about my complicated relationship with decision-making.

I've always found decisions excruciating although for years my unhealthy crutches helped to numb my fear of getting it wrong. I used food, alcohol and other substances and behaviours to change the way I felt and to manage my terror of making a bad choice.

From the outside, I looked like a confident, competent decision-maker. I packed a rucksack at 22, bought a one-way ticket to Sydney and worked my way around Australia for a year. From there, I travelled to New Zealand, Fiji, the United States and down to Mexico. I booked flights, found jobs, rented flats and chose a career in journalism, all on my own.

As a Reuters news reporter, I had to make decisions under pressure and to ridiculously tight deadlines. In a split second, I had to decide what former Prime Minister Tony Blair actually meant when he spoke to me and other journalists about the strength of the Chinese currency as his plane flew out of Beijing. I had to choose at what point to break out of the huddle of reporters and call my news desk and I had to know exactly what headline to dictate when the editor answered the phone. I had to do all that knowing that if I got it wrong, the traders watching their Reuters screens might shout 'sell' instead of 'buy' and the financial markets might move.

No wonder I needed food to cope with that job. I can feel my adrenaline levels rising just writing about it.

Bingeing took the edge off the fear but when I put the food down, the fear was still there. It was only when I tried to live without my crutches that I understood how petrified I was of life, of people and of making the wrong choice.

I would agonise over clothes or boots, over whether to buy

the brown pair or the black, sometimes buying both because I just couldn't decide. I would fret when booking flights, not knowing whether to land at Gatwick at midnight or Luton at eleven o'clock, or to stay away for eight days or nine.

The friends I would phone to talk through my choices said they felt exhausted just listening to me. How could I live like that?

With that track record, you can imagine that deciding whether to date a guy or not, whether to end a relationship or stay in it or whether to commit to a partner or go in search of someone else was almost unbearable.

In therapy, I began to explore why decisions caused me so much pain. I came to understand that ambivalence was my default – it ran through me like the candy swirl runs through a stick of Blackpool Rock.

I've lost count of the number of times I've used the phrase, 'I'm in two minds about it'. I almost said it the other day to my partner but then I stopped myself, perhaps for the first time ever. I was tired of hearing it, tired of stating the obvious. Of course I was in two minds. I've been in two minds about everything for as far back as I can remember.

Ambivalence, according to the dictionary, means to have contradictory feelings or opposing viewpoints about something. It's about uncertainty and fluctuation, particularly when it comes to making a decision or a choice. It's about being pulled strongly in two different directions.

I was young when I had my first experience of being torn. I was in the breakfast room of my childhood home, where I used to sprinkle spoonfuls of sugar onto my Ready Brek cereal and then eat the dark layer off the top before sprinkling on more sugar and doing the same again.

My mum was standing by the door into the kitchen while Dad was standing on the other side of the room, by the entrance to the hall. I was moving between the two grown-ups as they argued, edging towards Mum, then stepping towards Dad, unsure of which side to take, not knowing whether to wrap myself in my mum's skirt or cling to my dad's trouser leg.

The picture is a vivid one but I can't be sure if it happened exactly like that or if I've imagined the scene based on a strong childhood feeling of being split. Either way, I've lived with that feeling ever since. I've felt unsure, undecided and pulled in two directions. I've felt paralysed with fear at times.

I understand now that I also internalised ambivalence because I was treated ambivalently – sometimes cherished and sometimes ignored – so it became a natural part of life. Furthermore, I believe I have always struggled to make decisions and be happy with my choice because I grew up without a secure base, to use a term from psychotherapy. This means I didn't get the feeling of safety I needed from my caregivers to explore the world with confidence so I developed anxiety. I was a sensitive child and as I've said, I now identify as a Highly Sensitive Person – someone who is very attuned to their environment and to the feelings of others. I must have sensed that things weren't right at home, that my mum and dad had a rocky relationship and that our family was at risk of splitting up.

After Dad left, we moved to a smaller house, then a flat for a while, then a smaller house again. I was aware of not feeling secure and of not knowing what would happen next. It was as if I was standing on shaky ground – like I was trying to find my footing on shifting sands.

I became sensitive to other people's moods, learning to predict them and to respond in a way I thought others wanted me to. I learned not to rock the boat, to stay quiet and to keep the peace. When I did speak up, the adults around me sometimes challenged my view of reality and as a child, I naturally assumed they were right and I was wrong. From then on, I understood that I couldn't trust myself. I learned not to listen to my intuition. I learned to ignore any feelings of unease or doubt.

While I couldn't trust myself, I felt there was nobody else to rely on either and that wasn't a good place to be. That's why I turned to food for comfort and for stability. Sugar soothed me and alcohol empowered me, albeit momentarily. The extra weight helped me to feel more solid. Later, though, these childhood friends turned into enemies. I had to let them go but without them the world was a scary place.

My ambivalence was crippling when it came to money. As a child, I had a sense we couldn't afford the things we bought. I had a new tennis racket, a new sleeping bag to go camping with school, a nice bike and a beautiful red coat from C&A. I wanted them all so badly but at the same time, I felt a huge sense of guilt when we bought them.

This guilt came with me whenever I went shopping so the choices I made took on huge significance. I had to get them right. Big sacrifices had been made and I would only get one chance. I had to buy the perfect tennis racket and the right coat because I could never have another one.

As an adult, I have struggled to buy anything for more than 20 pounds. Should I buy it? Do I deserve it? Can I afford it? Is it the right choice? Will it last or will it wear out? I get in a flap over boots, running shoes, wetsuits, sofas and holidays, and once I've bought an item, I spend the next days or weeks regretting the decision I've made. I'm famous for it amongst my friends.

Just last week, I agonised over whether to buy a woolly hat that cost six pounds.

'It can't be easy being you,' my partner laughed.

'It isn't,' I replied.

Large purchases like the home we bought together cause anxiety spikes and many sleepless nights. I just don't trust myself to make the right choice. My ambivalence, my indecision and my lack of faith in myself have taken their toll. I'm sure they're responsible for many of my grey hairs.

Why do you think it's taken me so long to write and publish a book? I have 60,000 words of a memoir stored in one of my computer files. I've been working on it for four years but I just couldn't choose the right words. The only way I managed to publish *this* book was to set a deadline with an editor, announce it on Twitter, bite the bullet and push through the fear. Even so, I've lost sleep worrying about chapter headings and the cover design and wondering if it's good enough to put out into the world. It's excruciating. It's exhausting. But I knew it was time to wrestle my demons to the ground, challenge my self-sabotage and get the book done. I did the same in my relationship, but my inner saboteur put up an almighty fight.

Pause and reflect

- Can you relate to being pulled in two directions and to struggling with decisions, over big or small purchases or relationships?

- Can you connect that feeling of ambivalence to
  an experience from your past? Were you treated
  ambivalently or did you grow up without a secure base?

Facing the fears

We've established that I ran from relationships because I was terrified of being hurt. But I also ran away from men, found fault with them or kept guys at arm's length because I was scared of making a choice. Subconsciously, I deliberately drove men away from me by being controlling or by telling them to change because I was scared to choose one person in case I got it wrong.

What about all the other guys out there? What if I could be happier with someone else? What if I gave my heart to this person and shut the door to everyone else but then regretted what I had done? The entire process was fraught with danger.

I preferred to commit half-heartedly, to keep one foot in and one foot out, or a foot wedged in the door so I could run if I felt the need. I felt safe like that. But eventually, I understood that I could only love fully and reap the rewards of a deep connection if I put two feet in and made a wholehearted choice.

As I've mentioned, I ended my relationship with my partner some three or four times before we both finally decided to commit. It was my decision to leave every time but I felt I had good cause. Besides all the spurious, superficial reasons to do with his shabby flat or his windowless office, the baby obstacle stood between us.

Every time we got close, I'd raise the question of children, get the same answer, dissolve into tears and then leave. Surely I was just standing up for my dreams, refusing to settle for less than I deserved? I know many women who've done the same thing and who would do it again. In fact, I recently wrote an article for *Red* magazine about my relationship journey that was given the title, 'Why I chose love over babies'. Afterwards, I received a number of emails from women who had made the opposite choice and left a man because they wanted children and he didn't. Some of them emailed me in tears.

I understand it. I lived through it. I left too, but then I went back.

We each must make our own choice but for me, it wasn't as black and white as it looked. I was in my early forties so I had little, if any, time left to have a biological child. I liked the idea of being a mum and I hated the thought of missing out on one of life's great miracles and on that feeling of unconditional love for a child I had created with a man. I'm someone who likes to live life to the full, after all. Plus, so many other people were having families and they looked deliriously happy on Facebook, especially at Christmas time. My feed was inundated with photos of kids and parents all curled up on the sofa together with the family pet. I liked the idea of being 'normal', of joining the mummy club. Then there's all the biological stuff. I'd been menstruating since my teens. What was the point of all that bleeding if I didn't put my ovaries to good use?

I had also spent a lot of time working on myself and taking the steps outlined in this book. I had learned to connect to my feelings, to develop empathy for myself and for others and to be a better human being. I knew I was capable of giving love to a child and of creating and nurturing an extraordinary little person.

But I was in two minds – naturally. I had my reservations and some of them were similar to the ones my partner had. I was getting on a bit in years and wasn't sure how I'd cope with the tiredness, especially because exhaustion had traditionally led to a food binge. I loved my freedom and didn't like imposed routines. I felt my new life was just starting – a life of love, companionship, fulfilling work and a move to the seaside. I wasn't sure I was ready to give all the care and love I was finally giving to myself to someone else. I also had memories of my mum's struggles, bringing up two kids on a low income and not following her dreams, and it hadn't looked like much fun.

I could make the case that ambivalence robbed me of motherhood and if that were true, it would be a real shame. But when I was single, I never felt the urge to have a child on my own. I always wanted a relationship first and foremost. And I wouldn't say I'm naturally drawn to children. I love my nephews like crazy but I'm always delighted to hand them back and have some 'me time'. I'm also one of those extroverts with introvert tendencies. I need to retreat and have plenty of peace and quiet once I've been out in the world for a while. I wasn't sure how that would fit with having noisy toddlers.

As I recovered from my addictive behaviours and matured emotionally, I also began to understand that my hankering for a family was strongly connected to my past. When I looked at young mums and dads with their offspring and longed for a family like theirs, I was partly yearning for the unbroken, whole family I had wanted as a young girl. I was craving a happy ending to my childhood movie.

It wasn't surprising I felt so conflicted about motherhood

but I was absolutely sure of one thing – I wanted a life companion. I wanted to be in love. I was tired of being on my own. I wanted to be part of a family, even if that was a family of two.

Just before I committed to my partner, I did meet men who were up for having kids but the relationship wasn't right. When I was with them, trying to figure out if it could work, I kept thinking about the wonderful times I had spent with my partner and how content, loved, safe and free I had felt.

In October 2014, my partner and I committed to giving a relationship our best shot. I was in London and he was in Poole and I asked him over the phone what he really wanted out of life. When he replied that he wanted to be with me and to live with me, my stomach did a backflip. I felt the same. We agreed to put two feet in.

This didn't come easy to me. Traditionally, one of my feet had remained firmly out and the decision to commit sent my anxiety levels spiralling into the stratosphere. As soon as I'd jumped in, I wanted to row back. How was I going to do this? I would have to trick my powerful subconscious – that part of me that wanted to sabotage all my relationships and keep me safe – into staying with this.

I decided that I would tell myself that I only had to commit for six months and then, if it wasn't working, I could leave. For those six months, I would not think about or look at other men. I would delete phone numbers and cancel my subscriptions to dating sites. I would keep my eyes firmly fixed on the man in front of me, firmly fixed on the prize. I would not find fault in him. I would restrain my critical side.

I called in the cavalry in the form of my friends because I knew I wasn't strong enough to face my fears on my own.

I gave them permission to remind me of my six-month commitment every time I wanted out or mentioned another man's name.

They did a fine job. I remember walking down my street in London one day, beset with doubt and telling a friend down the phone that I'd decided my relationship was all wrong and that I had to end it. There was that guy off Guardian Soulmates who'd said he wanted kids, I pointed out.

'What if he's the man for me? Or what about … this can't be right. I'm not supposed to feel so unsure,' I said.

'May I remind you, dear Katherine, that you have committed to this relationship for six months,' my friend replied. 'Just give it six months then you can decide.'

Thank you, dear friend.

I took a deep breath, deflected any distractions and focused on the path ahead. One month turned into three and three turned into six and by that point, I was in love. I had suspended judgement and opened my heart to this man. I now didn't want anyone else. It felt like a miracle had occurred.

I packed up my flat, moved to Dorset and rented a room from a mutual friend for a while until I realised I wanted to move out of London for good. Gently, I floated the idea of buying a house together with my partner, making the point that I needed to find my own place to live. I then booked an appointment with a mortgage broker to explore the option of buying on my own – I was taking care of my needs rather than putting too much pressure on my man. By the second meeting with the broker, my partner was on board. Pretty soon, we were signing a joint mortgage agreement and getting lost together in IKEA.

I had called my own bluff and outwitted my indecision.

I had tricked my mind into committing and my heart had followed. My partner's heart had met me halfway. Of course, I had my wobbles. There were moments of doubt, times when my judgemental side returned with a vengeance or when I wondered about the Soulmates' guy who'd wanted kids. There were times when I convinced myself I'd got it all wrong. But those doubts always went.

What about motherhood, you may wonder. Not having children is a big deal. The truth is there are days, when my period comes or when I see a friend cuddling her toddler, that I feel sad I didn't get to be a mum. But all I can say is that right now, there's nothing missing from my life (although we may get a cat or a dog).

I am absolutely sure I am with the right guy for me and I am delighted that I made a bold choice. My only regret is that I waited so long and wasted a few years in indecision but I accept that was part of my journey.

Love comes easily to some people. They don't have suitcases of emotional baggage or irrational core beliefs that stand in their way. Love didn't come easily to me. I had to fight for my happiness and I had to choose love. I had to choose it wholeheartedly and with bags of courage.

If you get the chance, if it feels right and if you can discern between your intuition and your fear, I encourage you to do the same. Choose someone and see it through. Let go of the Ideal, wrestle through the Ordeal phase and come out the other side with the Real Deal.

You are more confident and more resilient now, more aware of your patterns, your blocks and your trigger points. You have strong boundaries and a healthy support network.

You have come a long way. You are ready to choose love.

Pause and reflect

- Have you had the opportunity to commit fully to a relationship but then walked away?
- Was your instinct protecting you or was your fear blocking you from love? How do you discern between the two? Refer back to Chapter 6 if you're unsure.
- If differences over parenthood have got in the way of a relationship, spend some time understanding your motivation for wanting a child. Be honest with yourself.

Leaps of faith

This step isn't just about making bold choices in romance, however. It's about making bold choices in your life. And maybe some of you will need to make bold life choices before you find love.

I did, although at the time I didn't feel as if I had a choice. I walked away from my secure Reuters job when Thomson bought Reuters and the offer of voluntary redundancy came my way. It was just months after I'd been signed off work with stress and depression and that money was a godsend. My mental and emotional health had been telling me to leave but I felt too financially insecure to make the leap on my own. Even with the redundancy, it was scary to let go of the status, the regular salary and all the cosy benefits that came with working for a multinational. But I have never looked back.

Look where I am now, finishing my first book in the Dorset home I share with my beautiful man, getting ready to walk on the beach as soon as I write the last line.

I meet too many women and men who desperately want

to make a bold choice, who want to change their lives, leave their jobs, move out of the city to the seaside or move from the countryside back to town. I meet people who are tired of dancing to someone else's tune or of paying the price of being too nice. I meet women who take their tears to work, who feel their soul go to sleep as they switch on their computers and who bury their lostness in bottles of wine at night. I meet people with wonderful dreams and amazing ambitions for their lives who don't have the courage, yet, to stand up for themselves and to fight for what they really want.

I know what it feels like. Believe me, I do. I have been there. But life is short. You know that. So don't wait until you have a health scare or a breakdown or the light inside you goes out to change your life.

Please, promise me you won't. Promise yourself.

Make a bold choice, or if it feels more manageable, take baby steps in preparation for change. Research new careers, spend a weekend in that seaside town you'd like to move to, take a month off work, get your flat valued or see how much money you've got saved.

If it feels scary, understand that it's meant to feel like that. It's supposed to feel uncomfortable when you reach for your dreams after years of neglecting them. Embrace the discomfort and walk through the fear. Take Mark Twain's advice: 'Sail away from the safe harbour. Catch the trade winds in your sails. Explore. Dream. Discover.'

My hope with this book is that you now feel better equipped to do this. My hope is that you feel more connected to yourself, stronger inside and more confident. My hope is that you are more aware of your blocks and have the tools and the courage to remove them. My hope is that you now have a clearer idea of what you want out of life and an understanding of what it might take to get there.

So muster all your strength, get all the support you need and then go for it.

It may be that you need to take a leap of faith in another area of your life before you find love. I had to transform my life in a number of ways first. I had to take the steps in this book and get back in touch with who I am at my core. I had to reconnect with the woman who loves to hike, camp, swim outdoors and cycle through the countryside for miles; with the woman whose heart needs space, the sea and a sandy beach to walk along every day. And I had to rediscover the writer in me.

So what is *your* heart's desire? Identify it. Then go after it. You never know, you just might find love there.

Step Ten: Reflection and action

- Write down one or two big dreams. They could be dreams of a relationship, a foreign adventure or a move to a new place.
- What small steps could you take to make your dreams more of a reality? Could you do some research, take a trip somewhere or start to save money?
- Close your eyes and imagine you're living your biggest dream right now. How does it feel?
- Trust that feeling and follow it. Trust that your heart knows best.

My reflections

Chapter 11

Reaping my rewards

*'When you arise in the morning,
think of what a precious privilege it is to be alive –
to breathe, to think, to enjoy, to love'*
Marcus Aurelius

My heart's desire was to write this book. I identified it and I went for it. I gave it everything I had. In the process of doing so, I found love.

Committing to such a precious and long-held dream and following it through to the end, despite my fears, was a huge act of self-love. But my love for my partner deepened also, as did his for me. As I buried my head and heart in my work, I felt his reassuring presence more than ever. He calmed and soothed me when my anxiety got too much. He brought me herbal tea, made lunch and dinner and picked up the slack around the house. He was my rock, my ever-steady oak.

Then, one week after this paperback went to print, he proposed at the top of a mountain in the French Alps.

Like any good romantic, I'd always wanted to get married. I'd watched a lot of Richard Curtis movies and had imagined my happy ending for years. But my partner and I had never had a serious heart-to-heart about it. Rather I had dropped a few unsubtle hints and had cajoled him a bit, while he had teased me, always jumping to his feet when he found himself down on one knee.

'I'd better not stay down here too long or you might get the wrong idea,' he'd joke as he swiftly tied a shoelace or picked something up off the floor.

I honestly thought he would take years to propose. He is a cautious soul who rarely rushes into anything, and there was no pressing need for a wedding. I imagined I would hold out as long as I could and then one day, I'd sit him down for one of those deep and meaningful conversations he so dreads.

But no, he proposed unprompted and much sooner than I expected. I'm convinced this book had something to do with that.

Yes, he had read the line in the first edition about us getting married 'when the time is right' but I don't think that's what persuaded him to pop the question. I think he asked me to marry him because I let go of any expectation that he would.

For two months, I immersed myself in this book, in its writing, editing, publishing and marketing. I was so committed to it that there was no space for anything else in my head – no room for thoughts of marriage and no energy left to try to hurry him along or turn him into someone he's not. And that's when he proposed.

I believe our heart's desires often come to us when we let go of them and focus on something else, when we stop trying to control things or convince others to do what we want.

So my partner asked me to marry him and I said 'Yes' but of course it wasn't as straightforward as that. I want to tell you the story of our engagement, and of what went through my head, in case you are ever proposed to or you are about to propose to someone and you're overcome with self-doubt, fear, uncertainty or a sense that it's not supposed to be like this. I want to share my truth to reassure you that there's nothing wrong with you, even if you do have doubts, and that ambivalence doesn't have to mean that you're making the wrong choice.

'Look, sweets, a ring,' my partner said as he took the squishy, red and yellow band from the Haribo packet, waved it in my general direction and then placed it hesitantly on the third finger of my left hand.

We were skiing in La Plagne in the French Alps and we had stopped for a hot chocolate at the top of a mountain pass called the Col de la Chal, a welcome rest after a morning on the slopes. I was still learning to ski. My partner and our four friends knew what they were doing. It was exhausting.

I stared at my jelly ring for a moment and then at him. Was he serious? Was he actually proposing to me or just fooling around?

Our friends, sat along the bench from us, looked over wide-eyed.

'Is this what it looks like?' one asked excitedly.

'It's not a proposal without a question,' I replied, taking another slurp of my hot chocolate and adjusting my sunglasses to try to hide the tears that had begun streaming down my face.

My partner held my hand and smiled but he didn't say anything more.

'Are you crying? Are they tears?' asked our friend.

'It's just the wind,' I said.

Sensing we might need some space, our friends shuffled along the bench and began chatting amongst themselves.

I looked at him and raised my eyebrows as if to say, 'So?'

'W … wo … wou …,' my partner said, struggling to get beyond the first letters of the word.

My tears kept coming but I wasn't going to finish the sentence for him. What if he didn't mean it? What if he was about to change his mind? That very morning he had knelt down next to me to fix his snowboard bindings, springing up quick sharp as soon as he was done and repeating that familiar line about me getting the wrong idea if he hung around on his knees for too long.

'I might just go to the toilet,' I said. Maybe I should give him a few minutes to mull it over, I thought. Or maybe I should stall him so he can ask again later, in a more romantic place and when we're alone.

But then he said it: 'Would you like to marry me?'

'Yes,' I replied without a flicker of a doubt, giggling as we tried to kiss each other over the wide wooden table and half-empty hot chocolate cups. 'Yes,' I said again, as tears continued to fall.

My tears were happy ones and I had a huge smile on my face but I could hear this nagging voice inside my head saying, 'It's not supposed to be like this.'

Yes, the scenery was stunning. We were over two thousand metres up, under blue skies and surrounded by snowy peaks. The ring was perfect too. Improvising with a Haribo sweet seemed fitting and cute. And we both knew I might have been disappointed if he had chosen a ring I didn't like. I have specific tastes, not to mention expensive ones.

I just hadn't imagined it like this. I had always thought

it would be just the two of us, but here we were on a busy restaurant terrace, within earshot of our friends and within view of a bunch of skiers we had never met. Where's my picture perfect proposal? Where's my fairytale? The child inside me, who had been brought up on a diet of Disney princesses, felt cheated out of her birthright. I thought about suggesting we move to a secluded spot and replay the entire scene under my direction, but I managed to stop myself. Had he even got down on one knee? I checked. Yes, he'd slid off the table.

Luckily, my joy got the better of my tantrum and I allowed myself to be swept up in the moment. I kissed my partner, hugged my friends, accepted hearty congratulations from random skiers and posed with my ring out on the slopes. And as we skied off, the jelly going soft inside my fleecy gloves, I finally saw sense.

Of course, the moment was good enough, far better than that in fact. It was a unique and fitting finale to our quirky, arthouse film. And how could I have expected anything else? When had my life ever followed the traditional mould? When had it ever looked like a Hollywood rom-com?

I had never been destined to lead a fairytale life. Few of us are. Show me the fairytale in which the father sits his vulnerable, eight-year-old daughter on his knee and splinters her heart as he tells her he is moving out; or the one in which the teenage heroine binges in secret on sugar and carbs. Show me the fairy story in which the leading lady despises her bloated body, drinks until she throws up and wakes up in a strange bed with a man she doesn't particularly like; or the one in which she kneels by her bed in the middle of the night and asks through tears, 'What's the point?'

In fact, given the first chapters of my life story, this outcome – a healthy relationship with myself and a proposal of marriage from a gentle, loving and attractive man – was more than a fairytale. It was a miracle. And if I could just get beyond my expectations of how my life *should* look or how our engagement *should* be or how I think I *should* feel in any given moment, then I would be able to truly appreciate the miracle of my life.

Could I do that? Could I give that gift to myself? Could I dare to believe that all was well and that everything was as it was meant to be?

I was getting there but I still had a way to go.

Back in Poole, a few weeks after our engagement, I sat at the beach, stared at the sea and cried tears from such depths that I feared my grief would swallow me up.

I cried because I was 46 and not 36 when my partner proposed. I cried because it had taken me so many years to get to this point. I cried because my life hadn't turned out as I thought it would. I cried because I had just bumped into a woman who appeared, from the outside, to lead a charmed existence – younger than me with a husband and two children and no need to work. I cried because it didn't feel fair that my life had been a struggle. I cried because despite our wonderful engagement, we would only ever be a family of two, perhaps three if we got a dog, or four with a cat as well, but a family without children or grandchildren to love. I cried for the life I would never have.

As I did so, doubt crept in. What if this isn't right? What if I'm making a big mistake? What if there's someone else? What if I could still have a family with another man? Surely if my partner was the guy for me, I wouldn't be feeling so devastated. I wouldn't be crying so much.

Fortunately, I have enough self-awareness to know that when my ambivalence rears its ugly head, fear is at the root. Fear is such a small, innocuous word, but it's so corrosive and dangerous – capable of sabotaging our lives and thwarting our happiness unless we can get a handle on it.

I was starting to get a handle on mine.

As I wrote earlier, I had learned in therapy that the closer I got to my heart's desires – to true happiness and a committed relationship – the louder my fearful voices would shout. I had learned that my inner saboteur would do its utmost to convince me to run away from love and to stay 'safe' and it would do so by finding fault with my partner so that I would never have to risk my heart and expose myself to potential hurt. I had also learned that honesty and vulnerability were the way forward. If I could find the courage to voice my fears, then I had a good chance of overcoming them.

That evening, I lay on the sofa in my partner's arms, took a deep breath and told him that I was scared – scared of getting married, scared of making a life-long commitment to one man, scared of everything that meant. He heard me in silence and then he said he was scared too.

And in that beautiful, intimate conversation, I realised how much I loved him and I saw, with absolute clarity, that I had to marry him. This man, this oak of a man, was capable, when it really mattered, of opening up his wall of a chest and showing me a glimpse of his vulnerable heart; of speaking his truth and sharing his deepest fears. And I knew then that whatever life threw at us, we would always be able to talk like this and there would always, always be hope.

Even the most magical of choices brings loss. When we agree to marry someone we love, we let go of all other possibilities. More importantly, we let go of our fantasies – those unrealistic ideas of the perfect man or woman and the perfect life that some of us have carried around in our imaginations since childhood. If we have already experienced a lot of loss in our lives, as many of us have, we instinctively will try to avoid it as much as possible. That is why we sit on the fence, never committing wholeheartedly to a relationship, or we self-sabotage, ending relationships that might have been good for us.

The key, as always, is self-awareness. If we can understand that we are afraid of loss and if we can do our best to process the losses from our past, to feel them and heal them, we will be more able to challenge our ambivalence, make a bold decision and embrace our choice.

As I continue to grieve the losses of my past and understand my fears, I am able to see the miracle of my life. I am able to feel gratitude for the fact that I have managed, against the odds, to form a healthy and loving relationship with a gentle giant of a man and that I have a wonderful partner with whom to journey through life.

The truth is that nobody has a charmed existence. Everyone experiences heartache and pain (some more than others, I grant you that). But we all have a choice as to how we live. The most important lesson I have learned is that I only have this life. There is no other. There is no 'could have been' or 'what if'. There is only 'what is'.

A good friend helped me to understand how precious life is as I wrote the final words of this second edition of *How to Fall in Love*.

Dear Tricia passed away in early January 2018 at just 53 following a short and sudden illness, leaving a huge hole in many people's hearts and lives. She was a fellow author who inspired me to share my words with the world. In fact, she encouraged me to face my fears, to write my truth and to finish this book in a message from her hospital bed just days before she died. You can read a few of her words on the back cover and on the first page.

Tricia made time for people and for the important things in life. She stopped to smell the roses and paused to gaze in wonder at the beach, the sea and the sky. She found miracles in the everyday.

We have no idea when our time will be up. So let's live courageously and love courageously, for our own sakes and in memory of those who no longer have the chance.

Final words

Congratulations. You have worked through the 10 steps and you are ready to reap your rewards, just as I have reaped mine. You have been on a journey of transformation, done some inner and outer work and are all set to date and fall in love.

Hang on. What's that you're saying? You've finished the book but you haven't actually done any of the work? You've read the reflections and the action steps but you haven't put pen to paper or downloaded a meditation app?

You're not alone. I've read masses of self-help and personal development books from cover to cover without ever pausing to do the work. The words have resonated with me but I've wanted to get to the end first. Either that or I've stopped reading halfway through and moved on to another book, thinking I'd find my answer there. I struggled to commit to one book in the same way I kept searching for a different guy.

If you've got to the end of this book without pausing to reflect or to take any action, can I suggest you return to the beginning? Can I suggest you reread it slowly and explore some of the points at the end of each step? Go gently. Don't take on too much. Spend longer on the steps that resonate with you most and do the actions that feel right. Work through the book over the course of 10 weeks or 10 months.

Ask a friend or two to go on the journey with you or sign up for one of my courses and do the work in a supportive group.

As you do so, accept that you're not going to get it right. You're not going to work these steps perfectly, come out all shiny and new and fall into the arms of your lifelong partner. You're a human being, after all. Remember how many times I made a decision to change and then went back on it? Remember how many times I hit my head against the same brick wall? Remember how I ignored my own roadmap at times and muddled my way through until I finally ended up in a relationship. It's progress, not perfection. Take whatever action feels right and then let go of the results.

You don't have time? You're too busy? You've got too much other work to do? Have a flick through Chapter 8 again and think about your priorities.

If you feel the steps in this book aren't right for you, commit to spending some time exploring other ways to do your inner work and to support yourself as you date or enter into relationships. Take a look at the Resources section or search the internet for something that suits you. We are all wonderfully unique so find what works for you. Or it may be that some of my steps resonate while others don't. As I said at the start, take what you like and leave the rest.

Whatever you choose to do, be prepared to transform yourself in some way in order to fall in love and stay in love.

I appreciate that *transformation* is a big word and the idea of it may seem ambitious or daunting. It may not sound much fun either. My intention isn't to take the excitement and romance out of dating. My goal is to help you get to a place where you can feel the butterflies, knowing you have chosen an emotionally healthy partner and that you are entering into a real relationship. You may need to experience some growing pains but joy is waiting for you.

But if you're sceptical about personal transformation and are looking for evidence that it can occur, look no further. The proof is right here in your hands – in my story and in the very existence of this book.

Over the last 14 years, I have transformed. I have let go of a series of crutches from food to alcohol to external validation. I have slowed down, filled myself up from the inside, left a secure job, moved from London to the seaside and fallen in love. I am still me, of course, but I'm a happier, calmer, more courageous, more compassionate and more loving version of me. A miracle has happened here, if that's not too strong a word.

This book is testimony to my transformation too. I look at the stack of paper on my office floor – a printout of this manuscript – and I can't believe I've come this far. Until now, I haven't been able to finish a book and release it to the world, although I have wanted to for four years or more.

I've been too scared – too scared of rejection and of criticism; too scared of what people might think of me or say about me, especially my peers. I've felt too much shame, a sense of being fundamentally flawed or not okay. I've felt I didn't have the right to put my truth in print (for some reason, I find it much easier to bare my soul on my blog than in a book). I've felt like I couldn't cope with publishing what inevitably would be an imperfect book, that I couldn't bear the embarrassment of seeing ugly clauses or paragraphs in the wrong place. I've felt like it could never be good enough and that I had to keep looking for different words (just as I kept looking for different guys). I've felt like I would need to resort to binge eating again to cope with the shame of being seen and to manage that sense of imposter syndrome.

But I've got here. I have matured enough to be able to publish an imperfect book, knowing that I'm now resilient enough to cope with criticism and mature enough to accept that not everyone is going to love me or my work. I don't need them to now because I love myself and I know I'll survive.

I am enough and this book is enough, in the same way my partner is absolutely enough.

Being able to accept this is a miracle in itself, a miracle that had me in tears as I drove through the Dorset countryside to see my therapist the morning after I wrote my final chapter. I had finished a book in time for my publication deadline. I had finished a book without stuffing myself with food. I had finished a book without abandoning myself or sabotaging my relationship. Yes, there was a period when I worked intensely like I had back in my Reuters days, getting up before dawn, writing until late and forgetting to go to the toilet. But we are talking a matter of days. I got to the beach every day except two, even if I only managed to sprint from my car to the sea and back again. I ate three meals and I went to bed every night, even if my mind sometimes wouldn't let me sleep. In fact, the only real casualty of my busyness was my lipstick – I ran out of my only one.

Something happened as I drove to therapy that morning – one of those beautiful coincidences. I heard the Welsh rugby union referee Nigel Owens talking on Radio 4 to Kirsty Young on the *Desert Island Discs* programme. I only caught the end of it but what I heard moved me. Nigel was talking about how hard it had been for him to come out as gay and to tell his mum and dad the truth. But he could no longer live a lie, he said. He had to be true to himself in order to be happy. He had to be honest and vulnerable in order to be free. He then chose the record 'I Am What I Am', sung by Gloria Gaynor, and as it played, I rolled down my window and turned the radio up loud, taking it as confirmation that I was on the right track with this book and with my work. I have been honest, vulnerable and authentic too and this has allowed me to be free.

As I've written this book, I've moved further along my own journey of transformation. I've shed some tears as I've relived some painful episodes. I've felt grief as I've explored the price I've paid for my dysfunction. I've smiled too at my dating mishaps. And ultimately, I've felt privileged that I've had the opportunity to transform and recover and that I've found the courage to share some of my story with you.

I trust that your transformation won't take as long as mine. I trust you won't have to cry so many tears, rifle through so much emotional baggage or hit your head against a brick wall quite so many times. I had a long way to go, and I still do. I am still transforming. But can I urge you to begin and to begin soon? Can I urge you to discover who you are at your core, to accept all of yourself and to sing along with 'I Am What I Am'? Can I urge you to go on an inner journey and to remove your blocks to love so you can form a healthy and loving relationship with yourself and with another, if that is your heart's desire?

Trust me, the rewards are incredible.

Appendix I

Ambivalence about motherhood

This is an edited extract of a post I wrote in December 2017 on my blog, From Forty With Love, *the day after I appeared on BBC Radio 4's* Woman's Hour *to discuss ambivalence about motherhood. I wanted to include it here partly because I believe I do my best writing on my blog – raw, real and immediate – and partly because I feel it sums up the journey I have been on and am still on, to some extent, regarding motherhood. You will be familiar with parts of my journey from this book but this post gives a more complete picture. Many of my coaching clients are women who are childless by circumstance. Others have been or are ambivalent about having children. Wherever you are on your journey, I hope this post resonates with you.*

Whenever I do a short radio or TV interview, I come away wishing I'd said things differently and made my points more clearly and succinctly. In most cases, I come away wanting to write, wanting to make sense of my thoughts by putting them down on paper or computer.

So here I am.

Yesterday morning, I had the privilege of being on BBC

Radio 4's *Woman's Hour* to discuss ambivalence about motherhood with presenter Jane Garvey and fellow guest Sian Harries, an award-winning comedy writer.

I've wanted to speak on *Woman's Hour* for a long time, ever since I began to find my voice through this blog and to write about things I truly care about: eating disorders, addictions and self-harm, recovery, dysfunctional relationships, loneliness, singleness, the missing baby, grief, commitment-phobia and, in recent years, falling in love.

It's hard, in a live radio interview of seven minutes or so, to tell the full story. And I'm not going to be able to tell the full story in this post either, but I'll attempt a précis.

For the first, say, 34 years of my life, I wasn't in the slightest bit interested in having children. I didn't feel a yearning. I didn't make any space in my life to think about them or plan for them.

I was too busy travelling and focusing on my career. I appreciate *focusing on my career* is one of those standard phrases people use about women who've been busy working rather than having children but my story is much more complex, as I imagine all our stories are.

I didn't think about children because a) they simply weren't on my radar and b) I couldn't imagine anything worse than being tied down by kids when all I wanted to do was travel, have fun and work. I had no notion that children could be fun, bring joy and fulfillment and open us up to incredible experiences.

The messages I'd picked up as a child, being brought up by a single mum on low funds, was that children were a ball and chain around your neck, that they curtailed your career ambitions, drained your bank account and kept you home when you wanted to be out enjoying yourself. In short, they ruined your life. That sounds harsh and I'm not blaming anyone. That's what *I* picked up. My brother has three wonderful kids, so he clearly didn't absorb the same message as me. But then I'm female and my mum was a single mum who did most of the childcare. Dad carried on with his life.

So kids were not on my agenda. Neither was a relationship for that matter. I understood, based on my parents' unhappy marriage and divorce, that relationships were a bad idea, that they ended in loss, misery and hardship. I picked up that men weren't worth bothering with, that I'd be better off on my own. I took that message and ran with it.

I focused on my career because I was an intelligent, capable, adventurous woman who picked up foreign languages easily, loved to travel and managed to get incredible jobs doing exciting things (foreign correspondent in Mexico and Brazil, for example). It was the natural thing to do. Why wouldn't I?

But I also focused on my career because I craved adrenaline, excitement, achievement and the approval of others. The adrenaline enabled me to numb or hide from my uncomfortable feelings while the approval of others went a small way towards filling the gaping hole I felt inside (the hole in the soul, as we say in recovery circles).

My low self-esteem and sense of imposter syndrome drove me to climb as high as I could so I could win as much adoration as I could, to try and feel better about myself, to try and feel worthwhile. Of course, no amount of approval or achievement was ever enough. The hole inside was love shaped.

Just as I stuffed the hole with food to try and feel better, I also stuffed it with career success and an impressive CV.

None of that actually changed how I felt inside, but I kept trying, doing the same thing and expecting different results.

As my mid-thirties approached and I spent some time in a good relationship, I began to think about kids. By this time, I was in recovery from an eating disorder, although I was just at the start of what would turn out to be a journey of transformation. I began to think what it would be like to live in an idyllic cottage by the sea with a loving husband and a few little ones. Suddenly, family life seemed attractive. It also seemed like a good way to fix the emptiness I felt inside. My craving for a family grew, which put a strain on my relationship. I needed to know. I needed to know now if he was 'The One' and if this was going to work out so I could get on and have the children I'd begun to dream about.

That relationship ended, for a number of reasons, opening the floodgates to years of grief and loss. My dad had died the year before and I hadn't paused long to grieve, jumping into a romance instead, so it all came tumbling out. I had what some would call an existential crisis: what's it all about? Why am I here? I had what could be called a breakdown – I was signed off my big journalism job in parliament. Instead of going to press conferences in Downing Street, I sat on my bed and cried.

So for a few years, I had no choice but to focus on getting well and working on my recovery. As my 40th birthday approached, I began to think more about the absence of a partner and children, hence the start of this blog and articles about 'dating with baby goggles on' (as opposed to beer goggles) in the press.

As I hit 41, I didn't feel ambivalent anymore about kids. I felt kind of desperate. Now my time was running out and

I didn't have anyone to date, never mind have a baby with. How on earth did I end up here with this amazing job, great CV and beautiful flat, but with no partner or kids?

I turned my baby angst into a project and began to research a book about it, which I called *The Baby Gap*. I got an agent, but I didn't get a publishing deal and I lost all my momentum. I still aim to finish that book, or a version of it. I tested my fertility, interviewed IVF doctors and women who'd had kids on their own by various means. I talked with counsellors about the prospect of becoming a single mum via IVF and ruled that out because of my mum's experience. I dated but nothing worked out.

As my recovery deepened and I worked through a lot of my baggage with an excellent therapist, I began to understand that the emptiness I felt inside was about much more than the missing baby, and that a child might not change the way I was feeling. In fact, it could make it worse. I needed to re-parent myself first.

I began to fill myself up from the inside out and create my own happiness. I learned to soothe myself. I reconnected with the things I used to love doing as a kid – cycling, camping and being outdoors. I began to explore a different, more fulfilling career. The hole in the soul got smaller. The craving died down. I became more self-aware.

At 42, I decided to stop over-thinking my life, shelve my baby angst for a while and date a man I found attractive but who didn't want kids. We had a wonderful time but I ended it after a few months because I thought I still wanted a shot at motherhood.

In therapy, I was starting to explore my ambivalence, towards everything in life and especially towards a relationship.

I understood how scared I was of commitment and of love because my first experience of loving a man – my dad – ended in heartache and loss. I also began to delve into my ambivalence around motherhood. Did I really want a child? Was I ready to have a child? Did my own inner child need more attention first? Did I just want a child to fit in and to feel like I belonged?

At 43, having failed to find anyone I liked more than my ex-partner and having realised I had my own deep ambivalence about kids, I went back to him and we committed to each other. Nine months later, I moved to Dorset. Less than a year after that, we bought a house together.

All the while, my therapist helped me keep my ambivalence in check. He helped me to see that I found fault with my partner and wanted to run away and find someone else because I was scared – terrified of commitment, of intimacy, of love and of potential hurt. He also helped me to understand that the baby obstacle that stood between us had been a convenient excuse to avoid getting involved and that deep down, I was unsure about children myself.

I'm now engaged to be married to my partner. I'm 46 and we don't have kids. Most of the time, I absolutely love my life. I love my freedom and I love my work. I get to write from the heart and I get to coach others to create wonderful lives and find love. I'm doing things I've always wanted to do but have been scared to do in the past. I'm using my voice. I'm speaking on *Woman's Hour* and at events with *Psychologies* magazine. I'm running How to Fall in Love retreats by the sea in Dorset and will soon run them abroad. I've published a book and I am writing another. Wow. It truly is amazing. And I mean that. I really do mean that.

Sometimes, when I walk down the steps to the beach and look out to sea, I feel so much joy I could cry. I created this life. I did this.

At other times, though, it doesn't feel enough. I see pregnant women all around me and I begin to question my life. How come I didn't get to do that? I'll never know how it feels to grow a baby inside my tummy or be a mum. I'll never have a family of my own, beyond our family of two (or maybe three if we get a dog). I'm missing out big time.

Ironically, I had one of my biggest meltdowns in a long time the evening before I was going on *Woman's Hour* to discuss ambivalence about motherhood.

To set the scene, I was already feeling hyper-sensitive. We'd been discussing Christmas, a time of year when I really feel the absence of a family of my own, the absence of our own kids in our own house. A time when I find it virtually impossible not to feel like my life is less than others' – smaller, less complete, less joyous – even though I know people with kids and families struggle with their own stuff and that nothing is as it seems on the surface or on Facebook. So I was already feeling vulnerable.

We then went to a drinks party. There were only seven other people in the room besides us, one was a gorgeous toddler and two were pregnant women. Suddenly, I felt like a green-eyed monster, like there was something very wrong with me, with us, for not joining in, for not doing the baby thing that so many couples do, for not having that experience.

Later that night, grief hit me like a fast-moving truck. It would be simple to say the grief was about not having a child but I know myself better than that. The grief was too big, the sobs too loud, the pain too raw to be about that alone.

It was grief for all the losses, for the fact that I had no choice but to spend years of my adulthood re-parenting myself and healing my past in order to get to a place to even have a loving relationship. Grief that I only got there at 43, not at 33 or 36. Grief that my partner and I hadn't met in our thirties, which might have given us time to change our attitude towards parenthood. Grief over my upbringing and my partner's early life experiences, which for some reason put him off parenting.

Sadness. Horrible, heavy sadness. That my life hasn't been *normal*. That I haven't had the chance to do the *normal* things that others do. That there's something I'll never know or experience. The tears and whirring thoughts kept me up most of the night.

And now that tsunami of emotion has passed, how do I feel?

Better. More like me again. Keen to finish this blog, get on with my work and then get to the beach. Excited about all the wonderful things I'm working on.

And ambivalent. Yes, still ambivalent about motherhood. Which would be funny if it wasn't a little bit sad. If you gave me the opportunity to have a baby today, what would I say? I don't know. I really don't know. I'm on the fence.

In preparation for my *Woman's Hour* interview, I did my research. I read an article about mothers who wished they hadn't had children. I checked in with honest friends who have kids. For some, ambivalence doesn't go away after you have children. I saw my mum in those articles and those messages from friends – loving us like mad, of course, but questioning, regretting perhaps, and wondering what if.

I read about drudgery, boredom, loss of identity, isolation, self-doubt, curtailed freedoms and never-ending sacrifice. I also read about the fireworks that go off in your heart, about a profound and satisfying experience, about a love that beats all other loves and makes you a better person.

So where do we go from here?

I clearly have more processing to do. Ambivalence is a difficult place to be. You can only sit on a fence for so long before it really starts to hurt.

The important thing, no matter where we are on our journey – with kids, without kids, still with the option or with the door now closed – is to try and make a choice, for the sake of our own sanity and happiness, and perhaps for the sake of our relationship, if we're in one.

If it feels the choice we want to make is no longer within our grasp for whatever reason (to be a mum or not to be a mum), we have to try and embrace where we are and accept where we've ended up. We have to grieve the losses as best we can – give them space and time – and then try and live with 'what is' rather than always chasing 'what if'. This choice isn't a one-off thing. We make it, then unmake it. Our feelings ebb and flow like the tide, but perhaps with every movement, we get closer to resolution.

If we're still deciding whether to try for motherhood or not, I believe we have to get out of our heads and into our hearts. I'm a huge over-thinker. I try to work stuff out. I'm a journalist. I do my research. I ask questions. What do you think? What did you do?

But the answer, I believe, lies with our intuition, with our hearts. And we connect to that sacred, wise place by quietening down and sitting still.

I was editing this book on the train back from London after my *Woman's Hour* interview in preparation for the second edition. I've always thought my first chapter went on a bit, but I was struck by how much sense it makes and how important that first step is. The answer lies in *stepping inside* and connecting to ourselves, in understanding what lies within – the fear, pain, grief, sadness, negative beliefs or fixed ways of thinking that are stopping us from moving forward with our lives. We have to feel these feelings to heal them. We have to be aware of them to change.

To read more of my blog posts – I have been writing from the heart for six years now – go to www.fromfortywithlove.com.

Appendix II

Love Ladies

When we step out with courage to do the work we feel called to do, we discover that we can make a real difference to others. This has been my experience.

I have had the privilege of working with some wonderful women who have trusted me with their stories and invited me to help guide them on their journey as they seek to have a healthy relationship with themselves and to form a loving partnership with another. They are my Love Ladies – the women who have taken my courses, come on my seaside retreats and joined my membership community. They are my pioneers and I'm very grateful for their support and inspired by their willingness to face their fears and to change.

I asked a few of them to share some thoughts about their journey so far for inclusion in this revised edition. These are their words:

'Apart from a few unsuccessful relationships with men who were afraid to commit, I've been single for most of my life. When you're so used to making decisions alone and having to be resilient in times of stress, admitting to yourself that there is still hope and a real possibility of a fulfilling and loving relationship is like opening up a tightly shut clam.

Katherine helps you to do that. She brings back hope into your life and gives you just the right balance of gentle encouragement, personal insight and expert coaching. Working with Katherine over the past 12 months has felt like having a soft blanket wrapped around me – a reminder that I'm not alone in this big, wide, overwhelming and sometimes frightening world.

With Katherine's support, I found the courage to proactively approach and start a new relationship with a caring and loving man. My eyes were open to all the pitfalls of my past and, for the few months it lasted, I was dating with an awareness I had never had before. The relationship evolved into more of a friendship in the end, but the experience reminded me that when I believe in myself and believe I'm attractive and have a huge amount to offer a partner, I can make things happen. I look forward to dating more this year and I feel more confident I will meet someone special when the time is right.' – Nina, 46

'It's all too easy to give up on love, especially if your love life to date has been a catalogue of disasters. But working with Katherine has given me hope again. She has helped me to see that for me to move forwards, I have to do some work on myself and understand my own fears and the patterns that I follow, over and over again. No wonder I always had the same results!

She has helped me to think, to really think, about myself, how much I have to offer, what I really want, and to think about relationships in a different way. She has helped me to understand how I project my often irrational prejudices on perfectly nice men. I feel lighter and more optimistic again and more equipped to make my dream of a healthy relationship a reality. Most importantly, she has helped me to overcome my fear of being hurt again.' – Michele, 55

'*I joined Katherine's first online course in January 2017. I found that while many 'love gurus' simply scratch the surface and tell you how you should behave, Katherine's work goes much deeper. She takes you on a journey, helping you to explore your patterns, fears and insecurities and to identify what you would like in a relationship. The focus is on building your self-esteem and wholeness rather than looking to someone else to fill a space. Katherine's work is as much about loving yourself as loving another. The Love Ladies community has given me a wonderful space of mutual support and belonging. It has helped me to build confidence in my own abilities and has definitely been a factor in encouraging me to pursue my desire to write. The work I have been encouraged to do on my inner child has been particularly enlightening. Katherine's honesty is heartwarming and allows others to feel that it's ok to share and explore difficult feelings.*' – Sarah, 53

'*I have found Katherine's approach to love, relationships and life so real and 'doable'. With this book, her How to Fall in Love course and the online community that I'm part of, she creates a safe, accepting yet challenging place to look at myself and my patterns and to discover what it is I really want from life. I've been working with Katherine since early 2017 and all of our work has been valuable. I have had my first foray into dating after a decade, which was really successful in deeper, more meaningful ways than before. I haven't yet met someone I am committed to but I'm hopeful that with the support of Katherine and the other amazing ladies who are journeying together, I will have a relationship in my life when the time is right.*

Katherine's approach isn't about quick fixes or soundbites. Her mentoring and support have given me tools for the long haul. I am grateful for the way she has helped me to stay grounded and true to myself – to my needs, to my longings and desires. These are important life skills, whatever the future holds.' – Elizabeth, 40

Resources

Books

The Language of Letting Go: Daily Meditations for Codependents, by Melody Beattie (Hazelden Publishing, 1990)

Meditations for Women Who Do Too Much, by Anne Wilson Schaef (HarperOne, 2013)

Codependent No More: How to Stop Controlling Others and Start Caring for Yourself, by Melody Beattie (Hazelden Publishing, 1990)

Facing Codependence: What It Is, Where It Comes From, How It Sabotages Our Lives, by Pia Mellody (HarperOne, 2002)

Facing Love Addiction: Giving Yourself the Power to Change the Way You Love, by Pia Mellody (HarperOne, 2003)

He's Scared, She's Scared: Understanding The Hidden Fears That Sabotage Your Relationships, by Steve Carter and Julia Sokol (Carter/Sokol, 2012)

Getting to Commitment: Overcoming the 8 Greatest Obstacles to Lasting Connection (And Finding the Courage to Love), by Steve Carter with Julia Sokol (Carter/Sokol, 2012)

Getting The Love You Want: A Guide for Couples, by Harville Hendrix (Henry Holt & Co, 1988)

Easy Does It Relationship Guide for People in Recovery, by Mary Faulkner (Hazelden Publishing, 2007)

The Gifts of Imperfection: Let Go of Who You Think You're Supposed to Be and Embrace Who You Are, by Brené Brown (Hazelden Publishing, 2010)

Big Magic: Creative Living Beyond Fear, by Elizabeth Gilbert (Bloomsbury Publishing, 2015)

Living the Life Unexpected: 12 Weeks to Your Plan B for a Meaningful and Fulfilling Future Without Children, by Jody Day (Bluebird, 2016)

Online and video resources

Gateway Women – a global online community for childless women. www.gateway-women.com

Listening to Shame, by Brené Brown [Online Video] bit.ly/brene-ted-shame and www.brenebrown.com

Meditation apps

The Mindfulness App
www.themindfulnessapp.com

Headspace
www.headspace.com

For help with addictive behaviours

National Centre for Eating Disorders
www.eating-disorders.org.uk

Men Get Eating Disorders Too
www.mengetedstoo.co.uk

British Association for Counselling and Psychotherapy
www.bacp.co.uk

Overeaters Anonymous
www.oagb.org.uk

Anorexics and Bulimics Anonymous
www.aba12steps.org

Alcoholics Anonymous
www.alcoholics-anonymous.org.uk

Workaholics Anonymous
www.workaholics-anonymous.org

For help with dysfunctional relationship patterns

Adult Children of Alcoholics and Dysfunctional Families
www.adultchildren.org

The Meadows
www.themeadows.com

Codependents Anonymous
www.coda.org

Al-Anon Family Groups
www.al-anonuk.org.uk

Sex and Love Addicts Anonymous
www.slaauk.org

Acknowledgements

My thanks go to my partner Bill for being such a wonderful, kind-hearted, supportive and patient man. You're an oak. Thank you for accepting me as I am and for bearing with me through my ambivalence, indecision, second-guessing and insomnia. Thanks for bringing me tea, making me dinner, filling up my car with petrol and making me laugh when everything seemed so serious. I love and appreciate you.

Thanks to my friends in recovery and to the faith and recovery communities that have supported me and shown me the way. Thanks especially to Beverley for helping me to grow up emotionally. Special thanks also go to my therapist, Paul Sunderland of Outcome Consulting, for helping me to identify and challenge my relationship patterns and overcome so many self-defeating behaviours. I have come far with your help and I am very grateful.

Thank you to my wonderful friends who have heard my dating and relationship difficulties over the years and who have trusted me with theirs and thank you to the women who put their faith in me and took my first How to Fall in Love course in January 2017.

Thank you to my mum and late dad for passing on such wonderfully creative genes and to all my family for your love, your laughter and for reminding me of what's important.

I'd like to thank my editor, Deborah Taylor of Book-Launch Your Business, for giving me deadlines, providing great feedback and guiding me through the publishing world. Thanks to my designer Briony Hartley of Goldust Design who created a cover that was absolutely perfect for this book and authentic to me. Thanks to my co-workers at The Old School House in Bournemouth for your encouragement and support and for setting me a ridiculous deadline that somehow I managed to keep. And a special and poignant thank you to the late Tricia Walker, author of *Benedict's Brother*, who passed away just weeks before this second edition went to print. You inspired me, believed in me, cheered me on and made wonderful suggestions. Your memory lives on.

Thank you to Harville Hendrix for your insightful work on relationships and to Melody Beattie, Pia Mellody, Brené Brown and Elizabeth Gilbert. You have helped me to recover and inspired me to write.

Thanks to all the writers, musicians, artists and other creative people who have challenged their fears and put their work out into the world. Every time I read a great book, hear a beautiful song or look at a painting, I feel inspired to get over myself and to put my own creations out there.

Thank you to everyone whose inspiring quotations I've included in this book and to the writers and performers of the songs I refer to, especially Jerry Herman for 'I Am What I Am', Paul Simon for 'I Am A Rock' and John Lennon and Paul McCartney for 'Step Inside Love'. For the movie *Dirty Dancing*, I'd like to thank the writer, Eleanor Bergstein, the Great American Films Limited Partnership and Lionsgate.

Finally, I thank God, the sea, the beach and the sunshine. You give me courage and keep me sane (more or less).

Next steps

Leave a review

If you enjoyed this book or benefited from it, please consider leaving a review on Amazon. They really do help to get the word out to other potential readers. If you would like to offer any direct feedback, do get in touch. Thank you.

katherine@katherinebaldwin.com

Work with me

If you would like to work with me, either through individual coaching or by joining one of my How to Fall in Love group programmes, workshops, seaside retreats or my Love Ladies membership community, I would love to hear from you.

I offer one-to-one coaching on dating and relationships and I take groups of women through the steps in this book. I also offer mid-life mentoring to anyone who is looking for support as they make a major life transition or who is trying to discover a more fulfilling path. Please go to **www.howtofallinlove.co.uk** for further details.

You can also follow me on Twitter **@From40WithLove**, on Instagram **@katherine.baldwin,** follow my Facebook page **www.facebook.com/KatherineBaldwinUK** or join my Facebook group, **Being Real, Becoming Whole**.

My reflections

My reflections

My reflections

My reflections

My reflections

My reflections

My reflections

Printed in Great Britain
by Amazon